Iris in the Snow

Carole Bystrom

Copyright © 2012 by Carole Bystrom

Iris in the Snow
by Carole Bystrom

Printed in the United States of America

ISBN 9781625090171

All rights reserved solely by the author. The author guarantees all contents are original and do not infringe upon the legal rights of any other person or work. No part of this book may be reproduced in any form without the permission of the author. The views expressed in this book are not necessarily those of the publisher.

Unless otherwise indicated, Bible quotations are taken from The Revised Standard Version. Copyright © 1953 by Thomas Nelson and Sons, New York.

www.xulonpress.com

Preface

In the beginning, as I told my story to special friends, I had no idea how it would unfold. God's consistent assurance of His love for me was woven into every portion of my life. Some very special people stuck with me through the worst of times and the best of times. As the years passed, many of my friends encouraged me to write it down, to share the message of God's amazing grace and intimate involvement in our lives. I thought a quarter of a century was a long time to wait before telling the story until I got to the end. Then I realized it had all started way before I ever got to the beginning. Perhaps unlocking my heart will open another's. Perhaps more will hear the music of the Maestro. Believe, only believe.

Callings

Icy winds whip the autumn sky to pastel percussion.

Pause . . .

Pale frost stills the meadow mouse.

Soft!

Melodies echo my name in the shadows.

Turn . . .

Dance with me in the silver vision.

Come!

Sail the skies on winged promise.

See!

Hope blossoms unexpectedly, defying the chill.

Reality!

Look! An iris is blooming in the snow!

Words . . . songs . . . melody makers. . . who can catch the stars as they skate across the November night? Who can ride the riddles in the wind? Only the dreamers dare; only the bride hears the chanticleer. Listen! A soft melody drifts in the night, a symphony echoes in the silence.

Long ago and far away in the shadows of past sorrows, in the chaos of broken dreams, the Master plucked notes out of the sky, fastening them quickly to His staff before tears of time could wash away the song. Gray Loneliness argued with Hope, shrieking insults, hurling ridicule and rejection in outrageous mockery. "Songs? Hopes? Dreams? Stuff and nonsense!"

Even so, the music of the spheres awakened, music not even centuries of logic can silence, music not even the most creative, most incredibly gifted artists and priests of the earth can imagine or program. That, of course, is what make it so profoundly special, so uniquely real, so elusively present. That is what preserves the melody. When the Conductor steps into place and raises His baton, He reveals creation. He is the Maestro. His music measures the magic; mystic memories awaken, and we know that this is good. We are the dreamers and the doers of the dream. We, too, are the melody makers. We move with the Maestro.

Wait ...

watch . . .

wonder.

Dreams are sleeping, stirring in the darkness.

Changes

My dreams had truly been sleeping for a long, long time, and their slumber was anything but peaceful. One autumn night my husband had come home and very proudly announced he was being transferred to Sacramento. For a number of reasons, things had been in a bit of a turmoil, and his promotion required a major shift. He had to leave right away, so it became my task to get the house sold, keep the kids on track, and " hold down the fort". "It won't take long," he said. I told myself he was probably right. The real estate market was good; our house was great, and God had a plan. The only trouble was, God didn't tell me His plan. People came, looked, made offers, and left. I gave notice at the school where I taught three times, only to dance around like an idiot when a deal fell through or escrow was delayed. "Escrow will just have to wait," Mr. Meyers chuckled. "The kids need you! We need you!" He was a wonderful principal who treated students and staff with love and respect. I truly loved my job teaching reading and drama at Magnolia Junior High. The kids were wonderful; the staff was like family, and leaving was very hard. Interestingly, escrow waited almost as if on cue. What didn't wait, but arrived without warning right in the middle of *Charlie and the Chocolate Factory,* was the hurricane that surprised California and me. I had no absolutely no idea a hurricane could pack such a wallop as far inland as Claremont. Wild winds whipped normally quiet streets into mini rapids as waves washed up into yards, lapping at driveways and doorstops. Raging gusts of angry wind grabbed at our roof and uprooted seven trees in one fell swoop. The kids were terrified, not knowing what would happen. It's funny now, but I foolishly stood out in our front yard screaming back at the wind, pleading with our young Monterey Pine, "Hold on!" In desperation, I called my husband. I had a hard time appreciating his laughter as he sat in his warm, dry apartment in Sacramento. "Handle it!" he chuckled. "Handle it! Handle it!"

Handle it? I handled it all right. I lifted my eyes unto the hills, searching for help, and found nothing but heavy gray clouds. Several trees had gone down, including the Monterey. We were actually quite lucky. They all missed the house and the neighbor's cars. The next morning I hooked one end of a heavy chain to the rear bumper of our yellow Toyota pickup and wrapped the other end around a tree trunk. One by one, I pulled each one of our tree friends to an upright position and staked them up with sturdy poles. It is amazing how well I could pound such big, heavy stakes into wet ground. "Hooray! Hooray!" squealed the kids, dancing around in the mud. "Hooray for you, little lady," chimed my neighbor. "Hooray for you, God," I sighed. The trees were happy; the kids were happy, and I was happy, dirty and completely worn out, but happy.

Amazingly, innumerable women hold things together on their own in the midst of hurricanes, flash floods, tornadoes, and other forms of nature's fury. It is certainly not unusual for them to keep things together while families are in transition. They make countless decisions and calm the kids while they deal with homework, illnesses, and one crisis after another. It is harder than it looks, however, and only those who have done it know "Handle it! Handle it!" just "ain't funny Magee!" Slowly, all the trees recuperated, and so did I. Like so many others, I had made it. Our house sold for the full asking price just as the 1983 school year came to an end, and, finally, all of us made it up to Sacramento almost one full year after my husband had accepted his new position.

Since relocation had taken so long, we assumed our new house would be ready by the time the kids and I made the move. Ha! Ask anyone who has ever built a house. It is anything but the dream we read about in magazines. Building the house is another story in itself. As it turned out, for the next six months we lived out of boxes in a rental house big enough for three. We were six. We were tired. We were crowded. One night we awoke to piercing screams, "Spiders!" None of us had ever seen wolf spiders before in our lives. While the small ones were only the size of silver dollars, the bigger ones were almost as big as baseballs. The gray, woolly monsters terrified all of us at first. We would pull back the covers before we went to bed and after we got up in the morning. Each of us learned to carefully check things like shoes and purses. More than one of us had put our feet into slippers or sneakers and shrieked as the enemy revealed another hideout. We were living out of boxes, and it was a riot to go into the uncharted territory of a dark garage, even in the daytime. Luckily, while we were waiting for the house to sell, I had sorted through everything and tried to create a system that would help everyone find personal belongings once were in our new house in Sacramento. I had marked boxes, listed contents and wrote "Fragile" on those that contained special treasures. When the movers arrived, I had watched as they loaded the big truck, trying to take note of the sequence as the boxes, furniture, toys, and tools filled the van. I was confident. I was prepared. I was ready for anything. It is safe to say I was even proud of myself. We would have very few, if any, problems finding things. I had packed everything myself, so I knew exactly where everything was hidden, except the spiders. Growing up in the San Fernando Valley after World War II, I was accustomed to black widows and scorpions but not these guys. I remembered the psalmists' words about treading on adders and wondered if they applied to spiders. I had never even thought about the possibility of new creatures in new housing developments in a new world. This was just the beginning of my enlightenment.

One beautiful morning I went for a walk along a bright little stream right across from the house we were renting. Excitedly, I discovered wild blackberries growing just about everywhere! I gobbled a few and ran back to the house to get a bucket. Wild blackberries! Yum! I made blackberry pie, blackberry cobbler, put blackberries on pancakes, stirred them into yogurt. This was Heaven! Then one morning as I reached deep into the vines to snatch the plumpest of all blackberries, a yellow streak jumped off a branch to my left. YIKES! There, in the middle of a huge, amazingly beautiful web glistening in the morning sun was an enormous yellow and black spider! It was as big as my fist! To make matters worse his buddy was less than a foot away. I did not know whether they were friends or foe, and I did not stop to ask. Black and yellow streaks screamed, "Caution! Yellow jackets! Bumble bees! Stingers!" I grabbed my bucket and flew back home, my feet barely touching the ground. Everyone laughed until his or her sides ached, even me. Poisonous or not, I was taking no chances. That was the end of my blackberry adventures for a long, long time. I wondered what other creatures had played peek-a-boo with me in the deep thickets along the creek I had been lucky. Later, I learned rattlesnakes also lived in the fields along the creek, lots of them. At certain times of the year, it was especially dangerous as the newly hatched young ones had not yet grown rattles and looked very harmless. Even though it was a frustrating adjustment, we made it through those early months. I even figured finding every single piece of my favorite china shattered was not too high a price for keeping our family safe and together. We had come through some very difficult times in the past few years, but we were all ready to make a new start. I had even managed to land a job right away, and things were looking pretty good. At long last, our big house on the hill passed inspection, and we were moving into our new home. We had spent countless hours picking out the perfect carpet, tile, and blinds, and it was all coming together. We were on our way, all ready to enjoy our new home and finally have some stability. I was excited. The kids were excited. Even Shin Tai, our beloved Akita, was excited. He seemed to know we were ready to start one more crazy adventure. He looked up at me, focused his eyes on mine, and lifted his paws when I told him to hop in the car. I could have sworn he was smiling, but an Akita never really shares what he is thinking. Shin-Tai and I were very close. We had raised him since he was eight weeks old, and I had crooned "Rock-a-bye-baby" to him so much he still thought he was a puppy. I loved him. He loved me. That was all he needed to know.

Plowing Ahead

*E*veryone was excited about getting into the new house, and the kids quickly established territorial rights. The rooms were spacious, so the girls shared the biggest bedroom while each of the boys claimed one of the others for themselves. As for myself, I had never seen such a huge walk-in closet in my life. Our room had French doors that opened to almost three quarters of an acre in the backyard. The landscaping was our next challenge. One by one, we made all sorts of little decisions and some big ones as things began to fall into place. There would be a pool and a spa. We would have fruit trees, lots of fruit trees. In all, we planted over a dozen, and I could see bumper crops of apples, oranges, lemons, almonds, apricots, figs, and tangerines. Along one side of the house we created a big vegetable garden in raised planter boxes. It was all very nice, but I really wanted some flowers. Right in the middle of all that sensible, practical self-sufficiency, I wanted flowers. "Later," my husband said. "Right now we need to get the corn, zucchini, watermelon, cantaloupe, green beans, and rhubarb started. Rhubarb ? I wanted flowers, lots of flowers. I needed flowers. In fact, I knew what kind. I wanted irises. Why I wanted irises was beyond me at the time. I actually thought it was my own idea. I had a premonition about the productivity of the vegetable clans and needed some small comfort in the endless canning I knew lay ahead. However, by the time all the vegetables were set and my husband finally agreed I could take time to plant flowers, every iris bulb in the country seemed to have been scooped up. "Plant petunias or daffodils," he snickered. "What's the difference? Flowers are flowers."

"No. Irises. Purple ones," I insisted, but by now they were all gone. It became a joke around the dinner table when I kept on looking for them. Eventually, the whole notion of flowers took back seat as we immersed ourselves in the endless string of things to get done. It seemed like life was going well, and we congratulated ourselves for having accomplished so much and making such a great new start. It had not been an easy task.

I had loved my job at Magnolia Junior High in Chino and treasured the people I called my friends. Getting older, it was not as easy to make friends as quickly as the kids did, especially when working long hours at my new job in Rio Linda. Every spare moment was spent putting things away, preparing new lesson plans for elementary readers, going to meetings, and correcting student papers. My own kids needed help with their homework; meals had to be had to be prepared, and chores screamed from every corner. Physically, I was exhausted. I was getting frustrated with the demands of a new house, a new job, and a new set of streets that changed names in the middle of the block. On top of everything else, the school district I was working for announced it would be phasing out its special reading program because of budget cuts, so all reading specialists would be going back to self-contained elementary classrooms. I had been part of an effort to identify struggling readers and pull out individual students on a daily basis for special help. The district's decision was a disaster for me because in addition to my reading credential I held only held a secondary level English credential. I was not qualified to serve in a self-contained classroom at the elementary school level. Just as I was about to panic, the principal of a nearby high school called and asked me if I would take a temporary position for the following year. Desperately, I grabbed the chance to teach, totally discounting the fact that temporary meant one year and one year only. The principal beamed and told me that with my track record something else would surely open up in the district. Naively, hopefully, gratefully, I took the bait, hook, line, and sinker. I looked forward to teaching high school as a great adventure. Excitedly, I worked all summer gathering appropriate materials and familiarizing myself with the district curriculum for sophomores and juniors. My friends in southern California offered advice and encouragement, reassuring me I would be just fine. After all, I had been on the cutting edge of changes in curriculum, student centered learning, and interactive lesson design. Moreover, everything I had tried with my students had worked for over six years. "Don't worry. You'll be great!"

Baptism by Fire

Wham! Absolutely nothing prepared me for the real life chaos and confusion I met that fall. First of all, since I was a reading specialist, the principal decided to give me a special class of thirty three juniors, none of whom had passed the proficiency exam, without which they would not graduate. On the surface, it seemed like a perfect situation. I had taught remedial reading. I had extensive training. I was enthusiastic. What could go wrong? What he failed to mention was that of the thirty, twenty seven of those remedial juniors were boys. For anyone out there who has taught high school, this has to be a real "gut buster". I had absolutely no concept of adolescent creativity when applied to avoidance strategies, nor did I even begin to understand their highly developed sense of teenage humor. The principal simply said many of the boys had a long history of academic and social difficulties, showed me the disciplinary referrals, and led me to my first class. My first period sophomores were delightful. Second and third periods went almost as well. Then we broke for lunch, after which it was time to meet the junior boys. I can just hear seasoned high school teachers begin to snicker and shake their heads. "Thirty remedial kids after lunch?" Right. I actually had the audacity to take my job and each student's educational needs seriously. I pulled out every trick in my little teacher bag, and they countered my every move with the skill of a Marine battalion. Each afternoon was a cross between *The Blackboard Jungle* and "Welcome Back Kotter." The girls and even a few of the junior boys were sweetly encouraging. The rest were absolutely unbelievable. I was stunned.

"Late? Whadaya mean I'm late? It's after lunch."
"Be quiet, lady. I'm talkin' to my homey."
"Read what? If l could read, would I actually be sitting in this stupid class?"

"Write? I can't write, neither. "
"I ain't gonna."
"I gotta pee! Now!"

Each day was more than simply another academic challenge. It was a physical, emotional, and spiritual marathon. Kids who are unable to understand what they read, unable to write, and unable to carry on a reasonable discussion in class carry an arsenal of defense weapons to protect themselves and each other. By the time they reach high school, many wear suspensions like medals of honor and are commandos when it comes to avoidance behaviors and class disruptions. Of course, I took my principal's advice literally and started writing out a daily stack of disciplinary referrals. Soon, I was asked to drop by his office and discuss my lack of classroom management skills. After all, it was imperative that these kids pass their tests in June, and it was my job to make sure every single one of them made it. Nothing was to interrupt the flow of necessary solid teaching and learning. Of course, I whole heartedly agreed. Of course, I had the same goals. Of course, I was whole heartedly committed to helping every kid in my class. Like Boxer in Orwell's *Animal Farm*, I would work harder, naively believing that would help. All the way home, I sobbed and prayed, trying to decide what tantalizing trick in my teacher training and professional development would tease them into even trying to read, write, listen, or think Collaborative learning, better known as working in groups, would be my next move. After all, students need to talk about what they are learning. I had attended many workshops, read several books, and thoroughly understood how non-readers need opportunities to talk about their ideas. At this point in time, the CLAD had not been conceived or discussed, let alone mandated. Small group discussion was a principle good educators recognized. There were people out there who felt a productive classroom environment needed to be a place where students could comfortably express their ideas, experience validation, and listen to their peers. Yes. Student centered learning experiences would be the ticket. A few stickers and stamps would work magic. Armed and ready the next day, my classroom management plan was underway full force. It seemed to be working! I was so confident! I didn't even flinch when Gloria called me over to her desk to point out what Matt had shot at her from across the room. Now, that was probably good because it took me a few seconds to realize it wasn't an ordinary balloon. "At least it's clean," I sighed silently to myself. Graciously, God arranged for the bell to ring right at that moment, but Matt stuck around just long enough to catch me turning a bright shade of flabbergasted fuchsia. The next day, just to make sure the fun wasn't over, Octavio suddenly threw a book of lighted matches into my briefcase. The whole class laughed wildly at once when I instantly dumped the water from Jillian's flowers into my pile of neatly organized sophomore essays. Dave and BJ came to my rescue, sopping up the water and cleaning up the mess. A few of the other kids automatically grabbed papers, separating each one and carefully laying it out to dry, making sure to blot up water spots to prevent the ink from smudging. "This one looks pretty good," Maria called out.

"This one, too," added Julie. Together all of them giggled and groomed the room in a matter of minutes. I knew better than to tell anyone what had happened. People would tell me my class was out of control, and I certainly would have agreed. I honestly didn't know what to think. As awful as they behaved, something about the wild bunch was warm and wonderful. In spite of everything they threw at me, I was getting attached to them. What would happen to them if they didn't learn enough to pass the proficiency exam and graduate from high school? What kind of life would they have in the future? I worried and wept. I waited and worked harder. Stickers, stamps, and kudos kept the kids on task, and, even if it seemed noisy at times, conversation was connected to the assignments. Everyone felt a little encouraged, including me.

On the day of my formal observation, I entered the principal's office as about as naive as I had been on the first day. Things seemed to be under so much better control from my perspective. Most of the boys who had been the most trouble were starting to get with it, and Ruben even asked me to help him with an assignment in his history book. Settling into the chair across from his desk, I saw a shadow cross the principal's face, betraying his wide grin. "So how is it going?" he asked.

"Fine!" I answered. "The kids are settling down and actually enjoying the class. What's more, they are even picking up some important strategies that will help them become life-long learners." I thought that particular phrase might earn me a few points. Instead, it had just the opposite impact. "My dear," he sneered, "these kids are not life-long learners. Half of them will end up in jail. In fact, just this morning, Danielle told her counselor she is three months pregnant. These kids are not here to have fun or enjoy the class but to pass their exams. Get them out of here. Furthermore, cooperative learning, pairs, partners, or whatever you call it is for elementary school kids. This is high school." He didn't mention the stamps or stickers. Neither did I. His message was clear. The coach was coming back to resume his position in the fall, and I was not going to be offered another position on his staff. From that day on, I did everything I could to teach my kids everything I knew they needed to succeed in life after high school. We read. We wrote. We filled out job applications. We created resumes. We read ads in newspapers for jobs and housing. We stopped at nothing, not even metaphors or similes we found in the sports page or magazines. "Ridiculous!" the principal snapped.

At night I wept. My husband just laughed and said maybe I just was not cut out to be a teacher after all. "Handle it! Just handle it!" was all he had to offer. Inside, I was in agony. No matter how hard I tried to put on a good front, I believed I was a failure. One day, I took my teaching credentials, my Bachelor of Arts and Master of Arts degrees out of the box where they were still packed. I put them in a pile on the bed and knelt down to pray about it one last time. I told God I would accept it if He really didn't want me to teach. Maybe I really wasn't cut out for it. This was obviously one test I had failed miserably. I no doubt deserved the disaster for being so confident in the beginning. My short-lived career was buried under a mountain of mud and debris. . . broken dishes. . . broken dreams.

Rusty Dreams

As if to accentuate my despair, angry clouds growled and grew darker every day. It rained endlessly. Long gray winter days had slid into a soggy spring. We held peace talks around the kitchen table as everyone tried to adjust to all the newness: new house, new friends, new schools, new schedules, new demands, new uncertainties. In the midst of all the struggles, I had not had time to lay in weekly supplies, so one Saturday morning we came up short for breakfast. I grabbed my jacket and headed down the hill to the store for pancake mix and milk, wishing it would just stop raining for one weekend. At that moment, the rhythm of the rain changed to a soft drizzle, and in the quiet mist, a melody from down inside my soul teased me into a smile. "Those April showers that come your way, they bring the flowers that bloom in May." Flowers... I had been too tired to think about them. In fact, if it were not for my fussy family, the gray clouds would have kept me under the covers just a little longer.

Pulling into the parking lot by the Jumbo Market, I noticed a line of tables clustered at the far end of a row of little shops near the post office. A banner drooped on the wall of the video store and whimpered, "Sale. Today Only." Curiosity tugged me toward the tables. It looked sort of like a garage sale without the garage or a rummage sale without the outgrown clothes. Actually, it was a collection of odds and ends, a community of clutter from someone's closet or back room. Then, underneath one of the tables I noticed three scrawny green arms reaching out from a rusty old coffee can. "Are those irises?" I asked the man who was putting things out and seemed to be in charge.

"Yes, mam," he nodded.

"How much do you want for them?" I mumbled as I began to fumble around in my purse.

"Why, not a thing, a gift, especially for you."

Laughing out loud, he lifted the dirty can out from under the table and handed it to me. His eyes sparkled, crinkling at my delight and surprise.

"I couldn't just take them," I sputtered, offering him a couple dollars. He just grinned all the more, refusing my money and waving me on my way. Needless to say, I raced through the aisles at the market and dashed home with my groceries and my treasures. That afternoon, I tucked the dilapidated irises into the soggy flower beds beside the house. "Those things will never grow," quipped the kids.

"Oh well, they were free," I countered. "What can I lose?" I really did not care if they laughed at me. I was too busy listening to the song that seemed to come softly forth from the muddy crib where the irises snuggled.

"Wait . . . watch . . . wonder. Dreams are sleeping." From somewhere, I knew I heard a faint melody, a song of hope. "By the time these bloom, things will right again." I hid the secret in my heart, and the rain washed it out of my memory. Every minute was filled with the stress of my job, the kids' schedules, and chores. Meanwhile, the tomato plants were in an arms race with the zucchini culture, and I was the appointed ambassador. More and more vegetables were beginning to ripen. "It's too early," I argued.

"Handle it! Handle it!" my husband teased. "It's great! Cheer up! I felt like bashing him over the head with one of those monstrous zucchini generals.

As the long, challenging school year ended, exhaustion, defeat, and depression almost swallowed me whole. Focused on frustration and failure, I felt God was teaching me a lesson, punishing me for being so angry, tired, and faithless. Dreams did die after all, and no poetic platitudes could paint it any other way. I had finished the race. I had no job. I was a total flop as a teacher.

Surprise Party

At least summer vacation shifted my focus away from the insanity of alarm clocks and tardy bells. For a couple weeks, I let the sun awaken me, and I would leisurely drift downstairs at my own pace to have coffee outside with the robins. One morning the phone hailed, jerking me back into the house. When I answered it, a nice lady asked if I was still looking for a teaching position. Suddenly, out of nowhere I was being called for a job interview! "Can you be here in an hour?" the secretary asked.

"Absolutely!" I almost squealed. I threw myself together, hopped in the car, and dashed down the driveway. In spite of the fact that I didn't know the way, I somehow drove all the way across town and made it into the district boardroom just in time. Pretending to be calm, I proceeded through each step of interview process. Inside, I was a nervous wreck. All the way home I told myself, "I should have said," and " I could have done so much better." No sooner had I reached home and walked -through the front door, the phone rang. It was the secretary at Mesa Verde High School.

"Can you be here tomorrow?'

"Tomorrow ?" I asked, dumbfounded.

"Yes. Our high school is on a year-round schedule, and classes have begun. We would love to have you start right away." Excitedly, yet ever so calmly, I told the very nice lady that I would be very happy to show up tomorrow morning. I wrote down the directions to the school, very politely thanked her, and hung up. "I got the job! I got the job!" Luckily, nobody was at home that sunny afternoon to watch me as I bounced from room to room. Bursting out the back door, I ran into the backyard. Rounding the comer into the side of the house, I stopped dead in my tracks. There they stood, a whole chorus of purple irises stretching upward on slender stalks, lifting their voices in one joyous melody. "Happy birthday to you! Happy birthday to you!" I had totally forgotten it was my birthday. "They're blooming! They're actually blooming!" I squealed. Nobody had noticed the tender buds. Nobody had heard the Maestro tap his baton, nobody except the orchestra. Coincidence? Some people may smile, others may smirk. Metaphorically minded or mystically mesmerized, I gave God my complete attention. All throughout that dark, miserable winter He had planned my birthday present. All that time, music was in the mud.

"Is that really you, God? Am I nuts? Was it really possible these beautiful flowers could be a message of love and hope and joy from you, just for me?'" Awe flirted with disbelief "Consider the lilies of the field, how they grow, they neither toil nor spin" (*The Holy Bible*. Revised Standard Version. Matthew 6:28). I knew the verse. Reason argued back just the same. I just could not believe it.

"Check it out. Go ahead. I knew you would." I could almost feel God's gentle hug around my shoulders.

The Quest

"*C*heck it out." The words buzzed around in my brain until they finally drove me to the library one afternoon about a week or two later. Of course, I knew flowers and folklore were old friends. After all, Shakespeare hid all kinds of secrets in his bouquets of brilliance. I started to look up the iris itself. Not only did I have little trouble finding information on the subject, I was soon captivated by the depth and complexity of this one small flower in particular. Culturally, flowers are often used to convey messages. As I thumbed through the books scattered on the broad library table, I soon discovered this one beautiful lily had been sacred for centuries. I had never thought of an iris as a lily. Many stories celebrated the melody of this one flower; in fact, one culture even deemed it "Messenger of the Gods." Indeed, irises seemed to have a spiritual component. To the ancient pharaohs of Egypt they were a regal symbol. Later, in the Middle Ages the iris became "the flower of chivalry, a sword for its leaf and a lily for its heart" (Blackadder, Kellaway 15). The three points of its leaf were reported to stand for faith, wisdom, and valor (Berry 17). Very excited, more curious than ever, I scooped up all the books and checked out the whole stack. I could hardly wait to get home, so I could open them again. One of the first things I discovered was that in ancient Greek mythology the iris was first named after the goddess of the rainbow. I remembered that God had set His rainbow in the clouds as a sign of promise, a covenant of His love. This was indeed an ancient melody, and the rhythm danced in my heart as I let the song weave its way through the corridors of time and into my tomorrows. Reading further, I learned the Greeks had described Iris as a brilliant, dazzling maiden. In her delightfully interesting book *Irises*, Susan Berry refers to her as "a radiant maiden borne in swift flight on golden wings" (11). Berry tells of a legend recorded in Hollingsworth's *Flower Chronicles* which reveals that one of her primary duties was to gently lead the souls of deceased women to the Elysian fields. As an act of faith, ancient Greeks planted purple irises on the graves of their women (Berry 11). To the Greeks, irises were the most precious of all flowers, and women had heard their beautiful chorus for centuries. But wait! Heaven's music was not for women only! In the Yemen mountains, Muslim soldiers carried iris bulbs with them to plant on the graves of their fallen comrades. Those valiant songs are still heard as the flowers bloom in fields where battles were fought long ago (Berry 11). It was not the flower itself that worked magic. What intrigued me was that people over the centuries had seen and heard the music of God's love and faithfulness. In my heart, I believe there is only one God, and God created this beautiful flower to speak to the minds and hearts of humanity. This one flower repeatedly speaks of love, hope, and faith in many cultures.

As I pondered all this, it should have come as no surprise that this mystical little flower had found its way into European heraldry. Indeed, John Gullum celebrated the iris in his *Display of Heraldry* in 1610 as the fleur-de-lis, "in Latin called the iris" (Berry 17). History records the origins of this symbol in the time of Clovis I, King of Franks in the sixth century AD. At that time, King Clovis was engaged in a fierce battle with the mighty Goths who had completely trapped him near a bend in the Rhine. The odds were against him, and it looked utterly hopeless.

Suddenly, King Clovis noticed some yellow irises growing in the water. He realized the irises could only grow in a few inches of water and ordered his men to cross. Later, when Clovis became a Christian, he adopted the golden iris as his personal emblem (Blackadder, Kellaway 25). Its three petals represent the Holy Trinity, Father, Son, and Holy Spirit. As time passed, the profound significance of this little flower appeared to be forgotten. However, in the twelfth century, the French King Louis VII restored its honor by adopting it as his own personal symbol during the Crusades. Thus, it became known as the "Fleur de Louis" or fleur-de-lis (Berry 17). In England it was called "flower de luce" (Blackadder, Kallaway 25). In France, the symbol stood for several hundred years as the emblem of a powerful monarchy. Then in 1789, the Revolutionaries of France obliterated it in defiance. Indeed, people were even sent to the guillotine for wearing a fleur-de-lis as jewelry or as part of their clothing (Berry 17).

In the twentieth century "flower power" almost became a household joke, but like many laughable lyrics, a kernel of truth exists, hidden in the strangest places. As a matter of fact, I learned that iris rhizomes have been used for a variety of medicinal purposes. In the past, orris root from iris rhizomes was used as a cure for blood and lung diseases, teething problems, freckles, complexion disorders, and face powders (Berry 18).

Searching with even greater intensity, this "lily of the field" continued its symphony in my soul. As I realized so many before me had heard its song, I no longer embarrassed myself by musings over my sanity. From my art history classes, I remembered the lily as a sacred symbol in many paintings and even sculptures. I began to look for specific examples in book stores and art museums in order to validate my memory. Many Dutch and Italian artists included the iris in their paintings of Christ and the Virgin Mary. This was to symbolize both the royal lineage of Christ and the purity of his mother, Mary. During the Renaissance the iris was often included in paintings as a symbol of the royal line of Christ Jesus. In his fifteenth century *Adoration of the Magi* Hugo van der Goes carefully painted three iris in the corner, two white and one midnight blue (Blacker, Kellaway15). Albrect Duerer's painting of the *Madonna in the Garden* in 1508 prominently featured irises (Berry 14). As the iris became a spiritual symbol for Christians, it was not unusual to find it in stained glass windows or carved on pulpits, prayer benches, or church pews. The root of the iris was also used to make rosary beads (Berry 18). Pondering all this, it is not difficult to see how many people began to view the iris as a symbol of the Holy Trinity, its three petals signifying three in one. All these fascinating factors filtered into my mind and my heart, challenging me to find a way to put them all together.

No matter how I rearranged the notes, the music and the message remained. The symphony in my garden was no figment of my imagination. Even so, I wondered, "Why?" I couldn't help it. "Why?" has been a part of my vocabulary from my earliest childhood memories. My teachers shook their heads in exasperation. My parents snapped, "Because I said so, that's why!" Whenever I ask God that question, I never get a straight answer. He usually says, "Wait." While I was waiting, I managed to misplace all the notes I had taken. So, years later, I would have to go back and find all this information again to document my discovery. A few days after my first trip to the library, I put all the books into a brown paper grocery bag, put them into the back seat of the car and lugged every single one of them back. The library was closed, so one by one I dropped them into the narrow slot and listened as they thunked at the bottom of the bin. Leaving the deserted parking lot that night, I clicked my headlights and checked for traffic. Looking up one more time, I saw them blowing kisses at me from across the street. Purple irises. "Lord, are you kidding?"

"Gotcha!"

Jubilee

Wow! Everything was coming up roses, actually irises. At this point, I am sure many believe the story has its happy ending, and I drift off into an amethyst mist, singing songs of praise. Part of that is true. For a while, I did bask in the glow of God's grace, grateful for another chance. I embraced each lavender sunset, nurtured each new sword that pierced the earth to reach for the stars, and sang many songs of rejoicing. At that point, I didn't even care whether or not anyone understood. I delighted in my momentary bliss, at least on the surface. Underneath, I was terrified. That is an understatement.

As I stepped before my first class of sophomores that morning, I was filled with fear and trepidation. Terror gripped me by the throat and barely let me take roll. The whole process would have been just a tad easier if I had any idea what to expect. Ten minutes into first period, Christi walked in strutting her pink Mohawk, leather jacket, mini-mini skirt, and spiky collar necklace. She handed me her schedule change as her boots stomped to an empty seat in the back of the room. My heart almost bounced right out of my throat. I pretended not to notice. Michelle had asked an intelligent question, ever so sweetly, just in the nick of time. I sighed, smiled, and answered her question, and the next, and the next. Right in the middle of this little skit, in walked the administrator who had hired me. "Take those sunglasses off, young man," she snapped, motioning to a boy a few seats to my left. "Mrs. Bystrom, please drop by my office on your prep." She turned and left. My stomach did a quick somersault, and my breakfast almost left.

Luckily, the bell soon signaled the end of that class, and I was armed and ready for my freshman remedial reading class. I would be very tough. I would be strong. As the early arrivals slid into the room and found niches in the back row, I sized each one up and calculated who might have the funny balloons, who might have the hidden matches, who might be waiting for the first opportunity to pick a fight. "Nope. . . nope. Not that one. . . nope. . . " They didn't fit the profile. They weren't the street wise, chip-on-the-shoulder kids I expected. They were young, sweet, confused, and waiting, ready to do whatever I might ask of them. They had pencils, notebook paper, and erasers, lots of erasers. No, they didn't throw them. They guarded them like hidden treasure. Mostly boys, they sat silently in their desks, eyes front, eyes shaded by hands that wanted to wipe away the whole scene. School was not their favorite place. Nevertheless, everyone was quiet and attentive, and some even asked intelligent questions. "Weird" I thought, waiting for the other shoe to drop. The rest of the day, whether I was meeting students in a reading or an English class, I knew I wasn't locked in a cage with ravenous beasts. I could do this, "Yes!"

When the final bell rang that day, I remembered to stop by the vice-principal's office. Maybe that was where the tiger was waiting. With Malox in hand, I popped two tablets into my mouth and knocked on her door.

"How's it going?" she asked.

"Fine, I think." was about all I could get out clearly.

"I noticed you have quite a bunch first period. Some of those kids have a real track record. How do you feel about your classes?"

After what I had endured with the juniors the year before, these students seemed wonderful.

"I think they are great kids," I smiled. Inside, I dreaded what would come next. "You have to watch out for Michelle. She's a real player. Don't buy into her drama. Just tell her to sit down and save her questions until you are through giving directions."

"I—I did that, I think." I stammered, trying hard to remain totally calm.

"Yes, you did. However, you asked her to wait. You did not tell her. I want you to practice telling students what to do, and hold your eyebrows down while you do it. You smiled. You totally undermined your strength. Don't smile. Eyebrows down. Mean what you say."

"Absolutely! Eyebrows down. I got it. Eyebrows down."

That night as I brushed my teeth, my husband asked how it went at school that day.

"Great!" I replied.

"So why are you scowling?"

"I'm practicing. Eyebrows down. Eyebrows down."

"Handle it." That's all he said, laughing at my silliness.

Jubilee

I tossed and turned most of the night, beating my pillow into submission, telling myself everything would be just fine. I was still scared, very scared.

The next morning, I arrived a half an hour early to be certain I was ready. Everyone was very positive and greeted me with smiles, hugs, and, "Welcome aboard!" I couldn't count the number of people who showed me around and reminded me to come to lunch in the staff room. The entire staff was so incredibly friendly; I almost thought I was back at Magnolia Junior High. People from the English Department went out of their way to ask me if I needed anything, and many took extra time to show me where things were stashed. The bell rang, and I dashed off to my first class in plenty of time to meet my students at the door. Princess Mohawk was already waiting at the door with her homework. Whoops! First error! I had really underestimated and greatly misjudged her.

"Thank you," I smiled. I unlocked the door, and thirty six sophomores tumbled into their seats. Every single student had brought a book, opened a notebook, and began to respond to the journal topic. I commanded myself, "Eyebrows down," and tried to scowl. I tried hard. All I could do was giggle and say, "Thank you! You're terrific!"

What can I say? They were wonderful. I rewarded them frequently with extra points or whatever seemed to fit at the moment. I even told them they would have twenty five extra credit points if they made it to the end of the semester without being tardy. Later, when I reminded them of that at the five week mark, Jason stopped short of spinning his gum in the air and said, "What?" He was in his seat, ready to work before the bell for the rest of the semester. That sophomore class stole my heart within just a few days, and they never gave it back. I came to love each one of the kids in my three sophomore English classes as much as I did my two freshmen reading classes, and I remembered exactly why I had decided to become a teacher.

Little by little, I would sneak in a group activity, terrified that the principal would walk in and catch me. Things were running so smoothly, one day I actually decided to present a vocabulary lesson with numerical prefixes which involved drawing and creating mythical monsters. I made it through second period and well into third before the door opened. YIKES! This was it. I was caught red handed, literally. My hand was red with ink from the overhead as I had finished demonstrating how to do the lesson. Mr. Basset, the principal, said nothing. He just stood in the back of the room and watched for about ten minutes. Then he circulated and asked the kids what they were learning. They told him. I trembled.

"Stop by my office after school for a moment," he whispered as he left. I don't know how I managed to get through the rest of the day. When the bell rang, I gathered up all of my courage and headed down the hall. I knocked on his open door, and he motioned for me to come on in and have a seat. He was very quiet. I thought for sure he would hear my stomach gurgling or notice how many times I was swallowing my heart.

"Decathlon," he said. "It's decathlon."

"Right, the vocabulary word meaning ten events," I explained, "in athletics."

"Watch the kids with their spelling."

"Yes, certainly," I stammered, afraid of what would come next.

"Wonderful! Simply wonderful," he smiled. I kept waiting for the other shoe to drop.

"Here it comes," I thought as he picked up his baseball cap.

"You really had them hooked. Every kid in the room was right with you. Can you do more lessons like that? Our kids really need this kind of thing. They need to enjoy learning."

"I'm sure I can think of something," I smiled back at him. He thanked me for stopping by. I wasn't in trouble! I wasn't in trouble! Back in the classroom, we did all kinds of reading, writing, speaking, and listening activities, but more importantly, we learned about each other. They were incredibly cooperative and accepting; I kept waiting for the trick behind the treat.

As Halloween rolled around, so did the harvesting at home. All those vegetables needed canning, fruit needed picking, and I was dancing as fast as I could to keep up with housework, homework, and schoolwork. One Saturday morning, the doorbell rang, and I answered it, still in my robe and slippers. Without makeup, my hair scrambled, I peeked out of the door to see Matt and Paul, two boys from Roseville High School, standing there with a dozen roses and a box of candy. Matt held a plaque someone had made in woodshop. "Super Teacher" had been burned into the wood. "Where did you go?" they asked.

"Here," I mumbled. "How did you find out where I live?"

"C'mon, we got our ways," he smiled. "Why did you leave us?"

"C'mon," I said. "You guys have all the answers. I flunked out."

"Hey, you were the best teacher we ever had! You were the only one at that school who ever even tried to teach us anything."

"Well, I didn't quite do the job, did I" "Hey! We passed our tests, didn't we?"

"Did you? Really?"

"Yep. All except Mario. He's in jail."

"But you guys hated me."

"You got it all wrong. You stayed with us all the way. We're really sorry we gave you such a bad time. It's just that you are so funny when you're mad."

"What?"

"Yeah, you're really cute when you're mad. . . and you loved us anyway."

" Did not. Did not. Did not." I thought to myself.

"Yeah, you did. Everybody else called us losers. We never would have made it without you."

"Who's at the door?" my daughter asked.

"Some of my students," I told her.

"See? We're still your students. These are for you." I took the deep red roses, the candy, and the beautiful plaque and closed the door when they said they had to leave. They were right. I did love them. "Cute when I'm mad is it? Eyebrows down! Eyebrows down. I'll show you cute!" I couldn't hold back the tears that leaked out of my eyes. "Allergies," I told my husband.

Meanwhile, back at Mesa Verde I had agreed to be the class advisor for the graduating class of 1989. That meant I would supervise candy sales, dances, car washes, and other fundraisers. It also meant I would supervise Sports-0-Rama practices, float building sessions, and put everyone back together on a daily basis. There were not enough official counselors to go around, so I found myself engulfed in one tragedy after another. Some of these may have been the usual dramatic ploys of teens in general, but many went way beyond the norm. There were broken hearts, broken families, broken bodies, unplanned pregnancies, and secret abortions they cried about after the fact. I knew where everyone lived, with whom they lived, and too many details to mention. I didn't ask; they told. As the months passed, they would open their hearts, one by one, as I held them, as I took them home, as I scooped them off of the floor. Within four years, I knew almost every student inside and out. During Sports-0-Rama practice, I would have two to three hundred students on campus practicing or painting posters. There were no administrators, no phones, no security officers, and no fears. I kept asking why we didn't have parent permission slips or some kind of parent contact list. This was way, way before walkie-talkies or cell phones. All went well, except for an occasional split head, broken clavicle, or bloody nose. After practice, I would take kids home because my old Girl Scout training would not let me leave even one unattended. It was a crazy, wild time. How did I keep up? I would pop Diet Coke or Pepsi one after another until I was bouncing off the wall with the best of them.

During Homecoming season, the kids, their parents, and I would spend endless hours building tissue paper forms onto elaborate floats and stand guard all night long, so no other clansmen would destroy our hard work. It was a time of frantic frenzy. On top of it all, it was even my job to drive our class float around the track on the football field and deliver it back to someone's house at one in the morning. When I got there and couldn't get the hitch off my truck, I was about ready to collapse in a heap when nice man came from around the corner. "Do you need any help?" he smiled.

"Whew!" No, I was not afraid of the stranger. By then, every big brother, grandpa, dad, or Uncle Joe seemed to know who I was, and I even recognized the nameless faces that waved as I made my rounds.

Those first years were so power packed, I hardly had a chance to sit still. I designed lessons, corrected papers, made materials, and even worked with another excellent teacher to write a grant to create a reading lab. I was also invited to join our district's writing specialist team and was warmly accepted. The teachers on the team reinforced and encouraged me at every turn. In fact, while I still attended every workshop I could squeeze in, I was beginning to be asked to present some of my lessons and strategies. I was thrilled when my evaluations were always "Meets or Exceeds"; finally, I felt like I was back on my feet. During all that time, one of the teachers at Mesa seemed so very supportive and eager to help, I really opened up and became very close to her. When we went to the reading conference in Anaheim, we sat like sisters on our beds, sharing hot fudge sundaes and secrets well into the wee hours of smoggy mornings. It was a wonderful time. She validated every idea I had, and she shared hers. Pretty soon, the kids even began to tease us about the fact that we sort of looked like each other. It was a sweetly appreciated compliment. We got our grant and set up a reading lab which supported every student who performed two or more levels below grade. Some didn't even know the months of the year. One day, we stopped Toby as he ran down the hall after his girlfriend. "Shannon forgot her bra," he said as he pulled it out of his pocket for proof. We shut the door and laughed so hard we had to come out to dash to the restroom. No, we did not condone their behavior or their upside down values, but we accepted each kid just as he or she was and worked very hard. They learned. They grew. So did I.

About the same time, Mr. Basset asked me to meet with another teacher to create a special program called Careers in Education. It was a new idea designed to help students explore their interest in teaching. While I was thinking about the whole idea, Marlyn, the teacher I was to work with, asked me to stop by after school. She said her husband had a surplus of some artwork he had to give away, and she wondered if I might have a spot for a painting or two. When I walked into her office, a smile splashed across my face. "I think that one is for me," I whispered. Right in front of the stack was a beautiful print of an iris in full bloom, a purple iris. Carefully, I lifted the iris and carried it back to my classroom where I found the perfect spot to hang it. Marlyn and I sat down that week and went right to work on the curriculum. She took it to the board, and with hard work, we actually got the class off the ground. It was unanimously approved and implemented the next year. It was so exciting and innovative that the board members came to interview us. We were even on television. The class was a remarkable success and continued to expand after Marlyn went on to be a vice principal and later a principal.

I stayed behind in the trenches. Our small course outline grew to two full volumes in the next few years. Eventually, I was coordinating students to be counselors at Sly Park, visiting elementary classrooms to observe and critique lessons, and helping with reading projects my students developed. It was like a teacher training course for kids, and it was really paying off. One of the most remarkable things was seeing students least expected to do well blossom into responsible teacher assistants once they crossed the threshold into their assigned elementary school classrooms. That sense of responsibility transferred into their general attitude towards others, into their academic performance, and into their lives. My students were not just recording and filing papers for the elementary teachers. They were designing and presenting lessons, reading with the children daily, helping those who struggled with math, and generally learning what it really meant to be a teacher. Our district had a special arrangement with American River College and California State University, Sacramento which offered scholarships to students who wanted to become teachers. It was wonderful to see my students actually pursue a career in teaching. The class grew in popularity, and I had students working in daycare centers as well as the elementary schools in our neighborhood. I had often dreamed of establishing a small preschool on our own campus, and I shared that vision with Mr. Basset and others. Eventually, my dream became a reality. Years later, another principal, Dr. Dennis Doris, brought a woman who had experience with the Regional Opportunity Program at another high school, and together we created the Careers With Children Academy.

Meanwhile, the three scrawny irises I had planted beside the house continued to thrive and bloom almost year round. I don't think they were supposed to do that, but they forgot. They would bloom when it was 28 degrees in the winter and 110 in the summer. We made the flower beds bigger, and I just kept rejoicing

The Round Up

The years flew by, and before I knew it, those precious sophomores I scooped up a few years earlier were now seniors. There was just one catch. Many were now failing classes and not expected to graduate. I could not believe it. I sent out spies to scour the earth and find out what had happened. Sure enough, they were failing, but that was not the worst of it. The same brilliant kids who lit up my world as tenth graders were lighting up other worlds, and guess with what? I was devastated. I was terribly afraid one or more of them would end up in ICU, or worse, the morgue. One morning, my friend caught me in tears and asked what was wrong. When I shared my concern for all those kids, she and I decided to create a Senior Girls network. We hoped to find out what was going on inside these terrific kids. We met with the girls at lunch and talked about whatever was on their minds.

Interestingly, the boys were on their minds. As we talked with a few, word spread. Before we knew it, our lunches grew from four or five to fifteen or twenty. The girls shared their dreams, their heartaches, and their insecurities. We shared our love and our combined eighty some years of wisdom. We laughed. We cried. We sighed. Through the girls, we found ways to reach the boys, and one by one we reeled them into our boat. Lunches were still for "Women Only." but everyone understood that. Were we politically correct? No. Effective? Yes. The boys were complicated. We called home when they were not at school and nipped at their heels. Of course, some went back to classes they had cut for days kicking, screaming, and shouting angry cuss words. Sometimes, I found myself wishing I had not been so brave. I wept as they kept making bad choices. I definitely knew too much. It scared me. I did not want them to fail; more importantly,I did not want them to die. I knew they were angry, but I could not sit by and let them self-destruct. One day in the hall, Bobby said, "Mrs. B, you just have to close your eyes. You care too much. Pretend it isn't there. Everyone else does." I could not answer him that day. I could not find a way to let them slip away. One day, I stopped Derek to ask him how he was doing. He was failing three classes! Derek had been one of the brightest of the boys in my sophomore English class. "Why?" I asked. Among other things, it turned out he had not done the psychology paper which was due the next day. He was ready to fail. I snapped at him and told him in my non-professional mother's voice, "That is simply not acceptable." I made him sit down in the library and begin to write. I told him he wasn't leaving until it was finished. He didn't argue. Somewhat dazed, he looked at me and complied. At about ten that night, he finished. Not only did Derek pass psychology and his other classes, he went on to place at the 98th percentile on his college entrance tests, and, eventually, he became a naval officer. I don't know where he is now, but I want to believe he is living out his dream, flying jets in service to our country.

As June approached, I was torn, joyous they were all going to make it, sorrowful they would soon all fly away. Remembering the Senior Girl's lunches and the in-your-face confrontations with those who wanted to give up, I wrote a poem and handed each one a little scroll. There was so much I wanted them to remember, so much I hoped they had learned beyond math, science, history, and English. They had accomplished so much and were crossing the threshold, to begin their own Hero's Journey. The little scrolls contained the following:

"Now It's Time"

❧

"Words... they're only words, but words are all I have..." The old melody drifts in and out of my mind as I try to play piano in the dark.
Words...
Notes...
Songs floating like soft rainbows against gray mists.
Rainbows...bright promises dreams.
Dreams...Treasure chests of hope.
Hope chests..
Treasures
You...
You are my treasures.
Through you I have danced the rainbow and touched tomorrow with my wings.
Through you, I have learned to hope, to trust, to risk.
Through you, I have learned to be honest...
    honest with you,
      honest with others,
        honest with myself.
Through you, I have learned what it is to be young, vibrant, alive !
Through you, I have learned fear is a shadow, a phantom!
I ride the arrow of light and you send me right through the middle.
Fear vanishes!
The child in me salutes!
The teacher in me smiles, remembering lessons I have learned at your feet.
The mother in me wraps her arms around you in one last tender embrace before those last good-byes.
Good-byes...
I am not very good at good-byes.
Letting go is not one of my talents.

Yet, it is time. I must set you free.
Be free!
Go, knowing you are all dearly loved.
Go, knowing of your beauty, your wisdom, your truth.
Wear your gifts:
Confidence.
Compassion.
Courage.
Comfort.
Choice.
Believe in yourself. See your successes.
Remember your strengths.
Crown your spirit with amethysts
In your dealings with others, consider circumstance.
Be patient. Be kind. Be crimson!
Forgive others for their frailties and failures
Forgive yourself. Show courage!
In your approach to the world, be brave.
Be bold.
Dare to set your sights on new horizons.
Don't settle for anything less than your best.
Be true to your integrity.
Dare to be idealistic, intelligent, invincible.
Launch your dreams into the clear blue skies of future generations.
Give comfort.
In adversity, strengthen one another.
Where there is strife and anxiety, sow peace.
Where there is despair, sow encouragement, hope.
Where there is loneliness, sow love.
Remember the power of your presence.
Let your silver light soar the universe on white wings.
Make choices.
In all that you do, remember you have choices.
Choose wisely. Choose life! Choose joy!
Choose to honor your body, your mind, your spirit
with virtue.
Have faith.
You are worthy.

Listen! The music is calling.
Join the circle.
Dance on the rainbow!

    Remember, God loves you very much, and so do I.

Somehow the whole crew made it across the grassy knoll, picked up their diplomas, and launched themselves into the wonders of new tomorrows. I stayed to train the next set of astronauts. Now, the class of 1989 would become seniors. I also knew almost every one of them way too well. I loved them as if they were somehow a part of my own family, and it was again very hard to think about saying goodbye. Change was everywhere. Our principal had retired, so we were starting up with a brand new leader just as my kids were getting ready to graduate. Ironically, saying goodbye soon became the least of my worries.

The Storm

*O*ne day the sky began to fall. Inaudible thunder rumbled across the horizon, and the ground trembled. All the lavender and turquoise colors spilled across tangerine sunsets, and musky shadows formed in the autumn sky. One of the senior girls told her mother that her very popular coach had crossed some universal boundaries. He denied it, of course, thinking no one would believe the girl. Other kids heard about her accusations and began to hassle her in the hallways, torment her in class, and generally give her "The Treatment." I found out through the grapevine, but I was not alone. Soon, another girl who had graduated the year before sheepishly appeared at my door after school, announcing herself with," Hi! Got a minute?"

"Of course," I bubbled. "It is so good to see you! How are you doing?"

"Not so good. I have something to tell you," she said, looking down at her immaculate white tennis shoes.

"What is it, honey? You look upset." I said, closing my door for privacy. As she began her story, my bubbles popped. Tears spilled as she recounted what she had heard about something currently going on at school, and then she dropped her own rock into the puddle. It had happened to her. Should she tell? Should she keep quiet? Should she run away? A dozen hard questions pebbled her heart and mine. This, indeed, was a difficult thing to live with, and telling would bring cruel responses from people who certainly did not want the windows in their world smashed. I assured her I loved her very much. I told her the seriousness of what she was telling me and the impact it would have on her and many other lives if she decided to reveal her secret. It takes great strength to stand up for what is right. Then she told me she had shared it. Her mother had come to the school when she was a sophomore and filed a formal complaint, but nothing happened. That is why her head had been down in my class so much that year. I sat there stunned. Somewhere from deep within my soul fierce anger began to build, but I did not share my rage. I told her I would love her, respect her, and stand beside her no matter what she decided to do. We hugged. Then we wiped away the tiny rivers of mascara that had cascaded down our cheeks.

The next morning, I saw her in the new principal's office. The next day in the hallway, I met the mother of the current senior girl who had filed the report. "My daughter is not the first," she said. "I understand there was another incident in the past." She held her composure, and so did I.

"No," I told her. "She's not the first. I just learned about it myself yesterday afternoon." That was hard enough. A few days later, there was another girl, then another, then another. I told each of them the same thing, reminding them that this was a very serious situation. They knew. I knew. Thus, the shadow that engulfed my world grew darker and more ominous by the day. One of my colleagues came up one morning and asked me if I had heard what these girls were saying. I confessed that they had only recently shared their secret with me. They were not cheap, wild and crazy "little sluts" as he called them. They had been student leaders and top athletes. He told me I had to tell them to back off, to say they were lying. It was ruining the teacher's life. "The man's life?" I replied. "What about the girls?" I stifled my outrage and just stood there, numbly realizing I was in this muck up to my neck. I had nothing to do with the fact that this situation had surfaced, yet I had no choice. "No," I told him. The attorneys, the social workers, and the judge would get to the bottom of it. The truth would come out one way or another. He did not like my response. I wasn't nasty and rude, but I wasn't a wimpy little mouse either. I held back my tears until I had closed and locked my classroom door. At home, my husband said to stay out of it. Nobody would ever believe those girls over the teacher who had been so loved and respected.

The weeks stretched into months as the girls gave depositions, took lie detector tests, went into counseling, and suffered the slings and arrows of retribution from those who could not deal with the harsh reality of betrayal and abuse by a trusted friend. In the end, eight girls came forward, and four decided to go all the way to court. They passed the tests. They sat on the witness stand and told their stories. It was not a "Kangaroo Court," but a serious, sensible search for truth. In the end, all the girls were vindicated, and the teacher was put on administrative leave. That should have been the end of it, but these kinds of things leave scars. Our school had taken a hit, and it would be a long time before it healed. The shadows began to growl.

Meanwhile, the new principal was making his own storms. A strict authoritarian, he told teachers, staff, students, and even parents every move to make. Most of us quietly acquiesced, but one of my friends dug in her heels and refused to be badgered. One day, when she did not respond to his immediate request, he pounded on the door and bellowed, "I am the principal!" I ducked into the bathroom, sat on the floor, and laughed until my sides ached. My friend just smirked. New rules forbid hats on campus, a very dramatic change. Our former principal, Mr. Basset, had worn a baseball cap every single day as he made his rounds. He called the kids by their names and knew every single one of them. The new principal didn't stop with the banning of baseball caps. The boys said he conducted strip searches when he suspected a student had illegal substances. One morning I saw an angry boy come out of the bathroom, rip off his shirt, and hand it over. "No, I'm not droppin' my pants," he said as he stormed towards the office. The new attitude caught most of students off guard as they were not used to being ordered around or asked to allow searches that most seriously invaded their privacy. Girls said they were not going to have a female administrator peek down the top of their panties. If they were suspected of having drugs, due process should have been followed, parents contacted, and protocol observed. It was not. I told them to tell their parents and make sure the situation was handled in an orderly manner. However, many kids simply stopped coming to school. Others rebelled in worse ways, and I found myself putting out fires on a daily basis. It was going way beyond just baseball caps, candy, and soda pop. One kid threatened to blow up the principal's car. Another threatened to jump him after school. "No way! You can't even dare to think such a terrible thing!" I protested.

We all kept trying to calm them down and told the kids there were orderly ways to discuss things and make their voices heard. Furthermore, they should have their parents call the principal or even the board if they had specific complaints. We told them which people to call and how to discuss sensitive issues. Over and over again, we reminded them not to believe gossip and not to break the law. Doing so would only ruin our reputation and hurt everyone in the end. I tried to settle them down and assure them that some of the things they were reacting to were rumors. "Listen to us, Mrs. B. They're not rumors, and you know it." I had seen enough to know they had many legitimate concerns, and my friend did, too. She was furious. So was I. She was brave. I was chicken. She smoked cigarettes; I popped Malox. My husband just laughed and told me, "Handle it. Handle it" My despair turned inward, and I began to get physically ill. One day when I was in the hospital for tests related to all the stress and anxiety, the principal ordered all the students into our cramped gym and began to recite the new rules. One of the boys in the bleachers had on a Mesa Verde baseball cap. The principal ordered him to take it off, and when the boy refused, the principal stormed the bleachers. Our dearly loved and much respected head football coach tried to stop him, but, within seconds, kids were pushing and shoving their way out of the gym and flooding out to the parking lot. They didn't much care who was in the way. The newspapers said our kids had rioted over baseball caps and soda pop. It was a total disaster.

Conquest

Meanwhile, things at home began to teeter. I felt sick. I was weary. My husband was always working late or traveling. He was almost never home. My son Bill had graduated from the University of California, Santa Barbara and found a job in the Bay Area. My daughter Cathy was getting ready to graduate from California State University, Sacramento. She had recently married and was starting her own life. My step children were getting about to leave high school and faced new challenges. The stress was building on a daily basis, and I felt responsible for the fact that my world was falling apart. In the garden, not one flower dared to poke her head out of the mud. My doctor said I needed to rest. My husband was scheduled to be home for awhile, so I asked if we could go to Yosemite for a few days. He said he didn't feel up to it, but I could go alone. "Are you sure?" I asked. It was totally out of character for me to go camping alone, but I had to distance myself from the intensity that surrounded every aspect of my life. "Call me when you get there," he said.

I drove straight through the rain all day, but I managed to get a campsite that night. Exhausted, I crawled into the back of our yellow Toyota and slid into my sleeping bag. I piled a few blankets underneath and on top of myself and snuggled down for the night. The rain pounded for awhile; then it stopped suddenly. All was very quiet. In the early morning, sunlight kissed me awake, and I opened the back of the camper shell to step out into freshly fallen snow. I hadn't even thought of the possibility that it might snow this late in the season. I wrapped my feet in plastic bags and hiked over to the store where I picked up a few groceries.

Yosemite falls roared, "Hello!" across the meadow, and I caught crystal kisses in the spray. The snow was not really that deep, but it was beautiful. This was my sanctuary. Sometime during that afternoon, I decided I would get up early and go for a hike. I packed a really big lunch and filled two canteens with water just before I climbed back into the truck and fell into a deep sleep. I awoke just before sunrise and headed out for Happy Isles where most of the trails began. At first, I thought I would just go to the top of Vernal Falls. The easy beginning turned into a staircase which clung to the ledges along the bottom of the falls. Rainbow mists that dance along the surging river have given the Mist Trail its name. Once I reached the top of Vernal Falls, I was surprised that I was not really very tired. It had not been much of a struggle, and I had made it without a hitch. After a little rest, I decided to go on up to Nevada Falls. That trail was much more rocky and rigorous. The switchbacks and loose rocks required some endurance, but the view from the top and the sense of accomplishment was worth the effort. High above the steep canyons, I watched the torrents leap from the top of Nevada Falls and gather again into pools above Vernal Falls before leaping into the valley below. I stretched out on the smooth granite boulders and rested, thinking I would head back down in a little while. Instead, I stood up and began walking further along the trail that led across Upper Yosemite Valley. The hike was level and remarkably easy. Tall pines, some centuries old, stretched their necks into a clear blue sky, and their strong arms waved to me as I walked across the open spaces. I stopped and rested whenever I felt like it. I laughed out loud as I watched chipmunks play hide and go seek, diving down into little burrows behind rocks or tree roots. I still had plenty of water and trail mix.

As I continued, I noticed a group of high school kids trailing along behind me. Why is it that teachers always get found out? While the boys went on ahead, two sophomore girls and I just sort of teamed up. They were all going to climb to the top of Half Dome. I found myself saying, "Me, too." After all, it wasn't that much farther through the trees that stretched along the vale. Eventually, the girls and I were at the bottom of a huge granite boulder. "Hey, that's really nothing," I smirked. I was right. That boulder was nothing. It also was not Half Dome. Once we conquered it, we found ourselves at the base of another boulder. This one had cables and some two by four boards attached to it. A bright red sign warned "Caution. If thunder clouds are visible on the horizon, do not begin the ascent." Clouds? We didn't see any clouds.

Starting up the cables, the strong young girls went first. Becky was the captain of her cross country team; her friend Marci was not quite as bold or confident. Although a healthy athlete, she had quickly tired. I watched her friend's ponytail bob as she went ahead of us, climbing boldly up the cables. I was feeling old and weak. I had tired even sooner than Marci. I could not believe how hard it was to pull myself up each segment as I gripped the metal poles. Moreover, I had managed to drink most of my water. "I can't do it," the younger girl cried. "You go on ahead."

"It's OK," I said. "I'll stay with you." At that moment, an elderly, but very fit, woman bounded down the granite slope. Her blue eyes flashed under her wrinkled brow, and a quick, stern smile crossed her face, "On your feet, Lassie! You've come too far to turn back now. Besides, look. Clouds are gathering. You've no time to waste!"

"Clouds?" I looked up. Sure enough, great thunderheads were coming our way and traveling fast. "Let's go!" I hollered. "We can do it!" We were indeed almost there, but it was not that easy. I pulled myself up one step at a time and wrapped my legs around one of the metal rods that held the cables. With each move up the smooth granite, I was even more certain this was it. I was going to die on top of this mountain. Another hiker offered me a drink of water, a pat on the back, and a warm smile.

"You're almost at the summit! You can do it!" he commanded. One, two, three, four, up we crawled. Suddenly, we were at the top. We had done it! My little friends squealed. I just stood there in awe. I walked all the way over to the edge, stretched out on the cold smooth granite, and dangled my feet over the ledge, too amazed to remember I was exhausted and afraid of heights. From ten thousand feet up in the air, I could see the forest fade into forever. Thunder rolled and lightning brought me to my feet. As I stood, I saw a big beautiful bird stretch its elegant wings to soar across an electric sky. It was far too big and powerful to be a hawk. "Is that an eagle?" I whispered.

"Yes." answered a deep voice beside me. I turned to see a darkly-tanned man with long hair standing beside me. Our eyes met for an instant and turned to follow the majestic bird as it soared in front of the menacing clouds. Before I could say anything more, the stranger was gone. Suddenly, I realized every single one of us, the girls, the boys who had gone ahead, and others were now standing on smooth granite, high on a mountain top, right smack in the middle of an electrical storm.

"I think we ought to get out of here," I told all the kids. Instantly, they responded to the reality of the situation. I bounded down the cables like a fireman, and the girls were right behind me. We were doing fine until Marci, the timid one, froze. "We're going to die!" she screamed as she clung to one of the metal poles. The boys, exasperated teenagers, purpled the air with fear and frustration, yelled at us, and high tailed it right around the cable to run down the slick granite slope. Thunder roared, and so did I. "MOVE!" I yelled at Marci, grabbing hold of the terrified young girl and jerking her from the post she had wrapped herself around. Together we all jumped, bounce by bounce, down the cables. Just as we hit the base, one and two-inch fierce hail exploded around us like ping pong balls. We hit the bottom running, stopping only long enough to quiet some horses now panicking where they had been tied. We were too frightened ourselves to be much help. Dodging the hail, we raced down the trail. Suddenly, a lone hiker came up the trail, headed for the top. His red hair and bristly beard were soaking wet. We warned him not to go any farther, but he brazenly scoffed at us, declaring he had hiked all day for this, and he wasn't going to let a little rain stop him. We kept running, soaked now from the heavy rain that followed the hail. Suddenly, the red-headed hiker came running back down the hill. "What happened?" we called out.

"Lightning! Lightning struck not a yard from my foot!" He zipped past us in a flash. Instantly, all our fear turned to exhilaration, and we collapsed under a ledge in a muddy puddle of hysterical laughter. We waited out the rain, laughing, sighing, half in tears, half in giggles. When everything settled down, I glanced across a little open space. I noticed a small purple flower nestled in a cradle of mud. There, with a flower for its heart and a sword for its arm, she raised her song in shouts of praise and glory. An iris? In the mountains? "Impossible!" I thought. "God, you are amazing!"

Yes. It was an iris. Later, I learned that wild irises cover the high plateaus and meadows in upper Yosemite. Born in the middle of winter, they are the first flowers to pierce the icy blankets of frosty snow. It is amazing that something so delicate can withstand such adversity to announce the glorious call of new seasons and bold new adventures. Although I didn't fully realize it at the moment, this particular adventure was much more than a walk in the woods.

I should have been exhausted by the time I arrived back in camp. I took a shower and settled down for the night. Later on, as I sat watching the campfire, visions flickered in the flames and danced with my soul. I had been to Yosemite dozens of times and never even thought of climbing Half Dome. Once or twice, I had seen a couple of the famous bears which routinely roam the valley floor. I had often stood quietly to watch deer graze in the meadow, but I had never seen an eagle. In fact, I had camped all over the United States and clear up into the Canadian wilderness, but I had never seen an eagle. This day, I had climbed to the edges of eternity. How did that happen? Why? Was it real? Could any bird play tag with a Sierra storm? I focused over and over on those precious moments on top of Half Dome. I argued with myself. Was it the altitude, dehydration, or my wild imagination? No. It was all real, very real.

The next morning, I scurried over to the nature center and asked a million questions, mostly the same one, over and over in disguise. I thought all the eagles were gone, especially in California. Ranger after ranger assured me I wrong, but I picked up a few books just to follow up. Soon I had plenty of evidence. I was not hallucinating. Of course, my next question was "Why? What did it all mean?" I know many people take nature's miracles for granted, especially if they are lucky enough to encounter them on a regular basis. However, God's miracles are amazing stories, for they are powerful and personal. As I pondered the whole thing in my heart, I remembered the words of Isaiah, "But they that wait upon the Lord shall renew their strength; they shall mount up with wings as eagles; they shall run and not be weary and they shall walk and not faint" (Isaiah 40:31).

Driving home, I was filled with hope as I praised God and thanked Him for the wonderful time He and I had shared on the mountain. I was indeed soaring on the wings of God's infinite love and incredible grace. Just to make sure I got it, He had even punctuated the day with a purple iris. Notice, it was purple.

I came back home and back to school with new strength and new determination. Somehow we all made it, and as I was called to the podium at graduation in June 1989, I shared my story. I told the class and their parents my hike through Happy Isles and up the Mist Trail to the top of Vernal Falls was like our first year together. They were new, and so was I. In a sense, we were all freshmen. It was a struggle, but we climbed each step with confidence. Our sophomore year was a bit more rigorous like the rocky terrain and nasty switch backs that characterize the trail to Nevada Falls. Once we made it through those bottom levels, we thought we were all "hot stuff." As juniors, we were even a bit more smug and hiked along at an easier pace. Little did we know what was ahead. Our senior year was like the climbing those cables that led to the top of Half Dome. Some stomped on ahead while others clung to the cables, gasping, "I can't do it. I quit. Leave me alone!"

"No, Lassie. You've come too far to turn back now," I announced, smiling to myself. Whatever it took, inch by inch, step by step, we all made it! We were at the top, standing on tiptoes at the edge of tomorrow. Like little eaglets, each one had grown strong and flourished in safety of the nest. Parents and teachers had even taken them on short test flights, "born on eagles wings" (Exodus 19:4). We had created currents of strong, sometimes invisible, support with our wings, currents designed to lift them and gently coax them into independence and adulthood. Indeed, like eagles, each one was born to sail through storms, rise above blizzards, reach incredible heights, and fulfill God's glorious purpose.

As I spoke on that warm June evening in 1989, no beach balls fluttered in the crowd. No bright confetti exploded on the lawn. Not one party horn squawked or screeched over the microphone. For a few special moments Wisdom and Wonder wrapped their arms around families and friends who had come to share their pride in these young people who had done so much and come so far together. They turned their tassels with dignity and decorum. Then the whole place went up in whoops and hollers that could be heard for miles. It was one "Hot Time in the City" for quite a few days. Indeed, they were not the only ones who were ready for summer.

Over the break, the eagle consumed all my free time. Once chores were done and everything was put away, rearranged, or thrown out, I began to sort out other things. By now, rejoicing with the flowers that bloomed regularly in my garden was a routine part of my day. A million other things screamed at me for attention. The eagle perched in the high canyons of my mind, waited, and watched. I found great comfort and security in many familiar phrases about the eagle in the Old Testament, and I deeply appreciated God's consistent reassurance that I would find my renewal in Him. This was not a new concept, for I had long ago underlined just those passages in my Bible. On the other hand, there was a new cadence building in the background, and though I briefly acknowledged it, I swept it aside. Whether or not I wanted to look at it that way then, the eagle has historically also been a symbol of much more than grace and comfort. For centuries, the magnificent bird has been exalted as a symbol of majestic power, strength, and leadership. It has adorned the shields of mighty warriors, accented flagpoles, and identified great ancient empires. Throughout the world today, it is an accepted symbol for freedom and democracy in America where the "Stars and Stripes" and the eagle proudly soar. The eagle is respected not only because of its unique size, tremendous power, and grace, but also for the regal image it creates when the monarch folds its wings, squares its shoulders, and raises its head. Even the appearance, structure, and function of the eagle's eye inspires much admiration. It is praised for its exceptionally sharp focus and depth perception; moreover, human beings who share the trait are often called "eagle eye". Moving from the concrete attributes of visual clarity, it is not very difficult to embrace the notion of spiritual vision as another connection. This is no doubt why Native Americans so often interpret eagles as messengers from God. No matter how long I looked at it or tried not to look at it, the eagle would not be ignored. It had announced itself and taken its position, alert and attentive, on stand-by. Although I had acknowledged its presence, I had to get on with other things.

Graduation day faded and passed as a bittersweet thing. It had ended a long established sense of security and a changing of the guard as young people moved away to start writing new chapters in their complicated journeys. Some went away to college while others married and began adult lives in new and exciting adventures. What I did not share with others were the new dramatic chapters being written in my personal life. All the while I was "fighting the good fight" at school, the struggles at home were tumultuous. Each year had brought new uncertainties, new challenges, and new heartaches. It's practically impossible to pinpoint when it all began to disintegrate because, in some ways, it all began at once while no one realized it.

Tremors

Before our move to northern California, we had faced many challenges as a family. We thought the transfer would give all of us a fresh start. We were continuing to make adjustments when, to top it all off, my husband's father began to act a little irrationally. At first, we all thought it was just his cantankerous personality taking a turn for the worst, and everyone tried to smooth over the gruffness and the unprovoked accusations. We were sort of glad to put distance between us and focus on rebuilding our own relationships. We had left my husband's parents living on their own in a little condominium we had bought a few years earlier. Nothing really prepared us for what hit that cold, wintry morning when the phone rang well before dawn.

"Come, quickly," his mother cried as I answered the phone. "He's going to kill me! He has a gun!"

"Calm down, Mom," my husband said. "What's going on?"

Crying, she told him she was terrified and that his father was threatening to shoot her. She said he had been yelling, screaming obscenities, and threatening her all night. Somehow, arrangements were made for her to get onto a plane and fly up to our house while my husband made arrangements to fly down there and figure out what had happened. When he met with his dad, the whole incident was just a blur. His father remembered nothing of what had happened and said his wife had left him for another man. It was all too crazy and too horrible to admit at the time, but his father was losing his ability to process things. I gathered some essentials, arranged to leave his mother with the kids at our house, and drove down to join my husband. He thought his mother was being irrational and repeatedly tried to tell her that it was all her imagination, probably because at that point it was what he wanted to believe. It would have been so much easier that way.

I spent the eight long hours on the road trying to figure out what we were going to do about these two fragile people whose lives were rapidly disintegrating. By the time I got to Claremont, things seemed relatively calm. In reality, it was deceitfully quiet and under temporary control. We had a friendly dinner and went to bed. Exhausted, I fell asleep quickly. In the middle of the night, I was suddenly startled by a click and a gruff voice commanding, "Don't move!" My eyes snapped open and froze on the dark steel barrels of a shotgun pointed right at my face. In silent panic, I prayed,

"Lord Jesus, if am going to die, I just want you to be real. Please, take care of my kids." That was all I could do. I didn't have enough sense to pray for safety or the wits to take control of the situation. Under the covers, I dug my fingers into my husband's arm and tried to wake him without being detected. He looked over at me and realized his father was standing over us. I prayed harder. The old man's hand trembled as he moved the shotgun barrel closer. "What are doing in my house?" he snarled angrily. I was terrified.

"Dad! Dad!" Quickly, yet sternly and in control, my husband sat up and talked my father-in-law into putting the shotgun down. "It's me, your son," he explained. I held my breath and didn't move a muscle for a little while longer. I just kept as till as I could, asking Jesus what I should do.

"Be still" He said, firmly.

"Yep!" I lay there without even a twitch, waiting, waiting. My father-in-law asked who I was and what I was doing in his bedroom. He thought he was still in his cramped little house behind the dilapidated apartment building he owned down in Los Angeles. Finally, he began to remember things, settled down, and asked if he could get us some breakfast. My husband just looked at me. We both knew the fridge was empty and the kitchen was a disaster.

"Hey, why don't we all just go out for breakfast? It'll be fun." I lied. We talked until morning, pretending to be calmly inviting him to come up for a visit. We told him his wife was waiting with the kids, and everyone was excited about seeing Grandpa.

The next few weeks and the months that followed were awfully hard on everyone, but they were only the beginning of a long and horrible ordeal for which we were totally unprepared. We rented a U-Haul truck, packed everything his parents owned, and moved them up to Sacramento. On the way, I was pulling a trailer for the second time in my life when a jolt snapped the truck toward oncoming traffic.

I gripped the wheel and straightened our little Toyota back into my lane. A grinding tug from the rear slowed me down as I pulled over to the shoulder of the road. Right behind me, my husband parked the U-Haul and came up to the window. I was shaking when he told me one of the wheels on the old camping trailer had broken off

"Whew!" It was a long, dark stretch of highway with no services around for miles. My husband went ahead to find help while I waited with the trailer. After the shotgun episode, I really wasn't afraid to be stuck on the side of the road by myself. His father was with him. They came back with a tow truck. A large burly man looked at the trailer, rubbed the stubble of his beard, and said it would cost about $1500 to get us on our way. Ha! I gave my husband a look he could not ignore and turned to the man, flashing the most polite smile I could conjure. At this point, holding back tears of fatigue probably made it much more effective. "Thank you so very much for coming all the way out here at such a late hour. Would you possibly know of a motel in the area where my father-in-law could rest? We'll call you in the morning."

"Of course, little lady," he smiled back. "I know just the place. I'll tow the trailer to the motel and pick it up tomorrow." I'm no math major, but I could see the dollar signs tilting in his eyes as he added up the road service, towing tonight, towing tomorrow, and whatever else he could think of at that point. We followed him to the motel, paid him for the towing, and got my father-in-law snuggled in for the night. I don't even remember the town we were in let alone the name of the motel, but I do remember the deep purple irises framed in the picture over the bed where I collapsed that night. Coincidence?

As soon as the sun came up, my husband checked over the trailer and decided the wheel could be replaced, and the axel wasn't snapped after all. "You're alright!" he beamed as he finally realized what had happened with the tow truck driver. He took the wheel to a shop in town, and within a few hours we were back on the road. I liked driving in the daytime better anyway.

Once we finally made it home, more challenges hit us at every turn. My husband's father was diagnosed with the beginnings of Alzheimer's, and his mother had no real understanding of what that meant. She herself was now diagnosed with dementia. Frightened and confused, her solution was to move them and all their belongings in with us. After all, we had a plenty of room, she argued. The boys could share a room and they could squeeze in all their furniture. Other things could be stored in our three car garage. In spite of her pleas, my husband would have none of it. Honestly, I was relieved. He told me to find a suitable place that would provide residential care for a reasonable cost. I searched everywhere for a place where they could be together. No one had ever prepared me for this phase of life or what I would observe as I traveled from convalescent hospitals to retirement homes. My mother had died from kidney disease at 44, and my father had passed away from bladder cancer and emphysema. Neither one had grown old, suddenly unable to make decisions for themselves. Since most of my childhood had been engulfed with my mother's illness, and daily trips to the hospital, visiting my in-laws was just a routine expectation. Eventually, we got them settled in together, at least temporarily. Every day, my mother-in-law would call, and I would go to help her out or just stop and check on my way home from work. Soon it became apparent they could not live together. First of all, my father-in-law was getting progressively worse, and medication to help the Alzheimer's just made him like a zombie. Then my mother-in-law became increasingly fragile and needed more care. I would stop by and make sure she had taken her medicine and clean her if she had soiled herself. At times she would say a I was like a daughter to her. During all this time her children were too far away to visit. She still wanted to come and live with us, but my husband said, "Absolutely not." He was tired of being a caretaker.

In a way, maybe it was all the focus on his parents that made his children react the way they did His son had always been very quiet and never really much of a communicator. He just withdrew more, claiming people were spying on him. His daughter, quite the opposite, reacted with her own set of behaviors, none of which I could confront without an explosion of emotions. I had raised these two since they were three and four years old, and after thirteen years, truly thought of them as my own. I had already struggled through the teenage years with my older children, and I recognized many of the same adolescent patterns. Still, nothing was working. It was one thing to watch my students self-destruct; it was another to confront these same issues at home. At first, my husband just laughed, telling me all kids experimented, had fake ID cards, and kicked up their heels. His sister supported the whole issue of " kids will be kids." They all sat on the couch and laughed at my "over reactions". "I don't want my daughter having a fake ID card and going out to bars," I protested.

"She's not your daughter! Leave her alone!" I could not believe my husband's retort. I was stunned, hurt beyond words, and left the room. As a Christian, I did not agree with him, but to say she was not my daughter after thirteen years was more than I could bear. I was deeply upset, but at that point, I really believed God would help me through this new group of storms. Taking care of my husband's ailing parents, keeping my own family together, and working full time demanded more and more of me. Each day, I went to work, stopped by to check on my husband's mother, and came home to start my chores. I did the laundry, cleaned up the house, and made dinner from scratch: lasagna, cannelloni, seafood crepes, chicken cordon bleu, Dungeness crabs. Nightly, I prepared all my husband's favorite meals; I wanted to be a good wife and a good mother. I turned to the only source of strength I knew. God had brought me so far, it never occurred to me that He would let me down. I read scriptures every night and clung to His promises like I had done so many times before in my life. I just didn't understand why it was not enough. I enlisted the help of other Christian friends, prayer chains, fasting, and anything else I could think of to find strength. My husband simply said, "Handle it. Handle it."

I could not handle it. My exhaustion let to tears; constant frustration led to tears; fights led to tears. Repeated daily confrontations with the kids led to tears. "They're not your kids, Carole. They're mine and don't you forget it!" When I suggested we seek counseling, he said that was fine as long as it was on his terms. That meant no "God stuff". I had to agree to a secular counselor. The meetings grew bizarre. I felt like I was totally alone. How could I explain that while I still wanted to be a good wife and mother, I need help to do the things I had always done on my own? During one session, the counselor adjusted his glasses, pulled his chair parallel to my husband's, and said, "If it is so bad, Carole, why don't you just leave?" I left the session, but I did not leave my husband. I went to my pastor for prayer and listened with all my heart when he said a woman must be subservient to her husband, especially when the poor man was losing his parents. He said that Christ calls us all to be servants to all men, putting ourselves last. Repeatedly, he assured me that God never gives us more than we can bear, and He would provide all of my needs. Each time we would meet and pray, I felt better for a little while, but often within a few days, something else would erupt. I tried to meet the demands of my job, the demands of my family, the demands of my husband, the demands of my faith. There was not enough of me to go around. I prayed. I cried. I ached inside, and neither scriptures nor sentiment soothed my spirit. "You are no fun anymore!" my husband sneered.

It wasn't too long before I began to get sick. At first, I just had stomach aches and headaches. Doctors prescribed different medications for stress, irregular heartbeat, and high blood pressure. One day, my friends took me home from school because I had terrible chest pains, and I spent the next day and a half in the hospital feeling guilty. My heart rate and blood pressure stabilized, but no one at the house had answered my doctor's messages, so they kept me in the hospital a little longer. The next afternoon I drove myself home, not really sure what to expect. Things were a complete mess.

Nothing could have prepared me for the eruption that followed over the fact that I had not taken care of the house, visited my mother-in-law, or followed my usual routine. When I asked who would be home for dinner that night, I was met with, "Who cares? When was the last time you cooked a decent meal around here?" Suddenly, there were all kinds of biting criticisms from every direction. When I tried to talk to my husband, he said, I was over reacting. When I prayed, he mocked me, finally blurting out that God was my reality, certainly not his. "Handle it, Carole!" It was one time too many. I felt like everyone, including God, had abandoned me. Handle it? I could not. The words of the marriage counselor echoed in the chambers of my mind. "If it is so bad, why don't you leave?" The more we tried to work on our issues, the worse they became. Moreover, old wounds from years before burst open. What I had tried so hard to bury and forget erupted, tearing at my soul. There were fights, cruel admissions, smart remarks. One night, after trying to discuss very painful, unforgivable, past behaviors, my husband sneered, "So just what do you think you are going to do about it? Who's going to believe you?"

Terrified and broken, I ran. I left. I had no plan. I had no money. I had nowhere to go. I just left. Suddenly, I had crossed whatever line had been drawn in the sand, and I left. For the next several hours I drove around mindlessly. When it got dark, I pulled into a campground and cried myself to sleep. "God, why have you forsaken me?" I prayed, "Why?" In the morning I found a place to rent even though

I had nothing to put in it. It was better than sleeping in the truck. At least I had a bathroom.

Later that day, I went back to the house to get a few things and was relieved that no one was home. Everyone had gone on with the routine as if everything were the same. I called and told them I would be needing a bed, some blankets, and personal items, but nobody believed me. The dissolution process was beginning. It would take years to complete. If I thought I cried before, it would be nothing compared to the torrents that swept me into despair over the next few weeks. I tried to work. I tried to function. Somehow, I kept on going, meeting needs of my classes and those of the graduating class I had sponsored for four years.

For the first few weeks or so, my husband would often call me at work, apologize, even tell me he loved me, but he would not admit we had a major problem as a couple or a family. Certain things just could not be openly discussed. Indeed, some secrets are better left just that, secrets. He said I was just overly emotional. I was against the wall. I was alone. I had failed everyone: my husband, my children, and most of all God. Finally, my husband announced he was tired of trying to pretend he loved me. "You're a nice lady, but you are just no fun anymore. It's over."

Severance

❧

The attorney said everything would have to be divided equally, and within a couple of weeks the house was sold; the trailer was sold; the boat was sold. Within a few more weeks, our faithful Akita Shin Tai was so "out of control" my husband insisted the dog had to be put down. He had never been a problem in all the years we had him, and I could not accept the need for him to be destroyed. "I'll take him," I protested.

"No, you cannot have him," he answered. "He's dangerous

"No," I said, "he's not dangerous. He's confused and very upset."

"It's already done, Carole." Click. More tears.

In my heart, I knew it was part of the liquidation process. My husband sent a check for my half of the profits from the boat and the tent trailer with one additional penny added for effect. My attorney gave me an incredulous look and asked again if I was sure I did not want alimony. I said, "No." I wished I had said, " No" to many other things long ago.

Right in the middle of all this, I went to school one day and found my friend had taken all of her things out of the reading lab we shared. It was still spring, but she said she was getting ready for the fall before we broke for the summer. I was so naive. All the while she was pretending to understand, pretending to comfort and encourage me, I had no idea that our friendship was over. My endless tears became fodder for fun and ridicule, but I didn't know it until I heard her openly laughing and talking about me in the staff lunchroom with another teacher. "We are getting a divorce. Carole just likes to masturbate in her pain."

"Ouch!"

To make matters even worse, she began to spread sweet secrets we had shared over hot fudge sundaes into a thick paste of pretended pathos. She shaped the bread of betrayal into delightful canapes, dusted them with arsenic, and served them at her whim at lunch, over coffee, at the Xerox machine, or wherever someone might venture into her realm. One by one, bite by bite, all the tidbits came back to me, spiced with lies. While I hadn't committed any horrific offense against humanity, I had foolishly trusted her with private heartaches, and in my weakness I had exposed myself to treachery. She was stabbing me in the back, and she knew it. She even smiled in the process. I never hinted I knew what she was doing. I didn't know how to cope with it. It complicated everything I was dealing with and pierced my soul. She knew exactly what she was doing. So did I.

Now I had a new lesson to learn. No husband. No family. No friend. I felt utterly betrayed and abandoned by every one in every corner of my life. I would not cry. Not this time. I would not tell her all I had heard. I would not tell anyone. I would hold my head high, smile, and give my very best ever graduation speech. I would pretend that I was lovable and capable, that God loved me, and life went on after divorce, betrayal, and defeat. At the same time, I was sure it did not. God had not answered my prayers. He had not rescued me. He had not healed my marriage. I truly believed He, too, was completely disgusted with me. Counseling was a complete disaster, and I had no hope left. At school, I pretended I was adjusting, that I was going to make it through and be all right. Privately, I was totally falling deeper into despair and began to question whether or not I wanted to live. I thought I had no such right. Somehow, I had enough sanity left to call my doctor and tell him exactly where I was emotionally. I desperately needed some help. God was gone. Maybe the secular world could help me. Humiliated beyond despair, I checked myself into the psychiatric hospital, turned over all my medications, and admitted I was lost, really lost. I felt totally alone. In my eyes, I was a total failure as a wife, mother, teacher, friend. The world would be better off without me.

Individual and group counseling were part of the daily routine. It was horrible. After one long group session, I ran from the room when someone said God was nothing more than a convenient crutch for those too weak to stand on their own. If God were real, why hadn't He honored His promises? "If your God is so real, so great, where is he now? Why is your world falling apart more each day?" The words stung. They were right. I was a fool to believe. I ran sobbing down a long green corridor. Turning into an empty room hidden behind two big, heavy, oak doors, I closed them behind me. I fell into the overstuffed couch, muffling my sobs in the great cushions. I don't remember how long I was there or why no one came to find me. When I finally got myself half way back together, I looked up, stunned, ashamed, and overwhelmed. There over the sofa hung two matching oil paintings, wide fields of purple and lavender, iridescent irises. I didn't want to look, yet I could not ignore reality. I did not understand. Flowers. . . they could not matter. I had failed Him. Nevertheless, those purple irises were staring me down. God was right there with me, trying to tell me He loved me. I had deserted my marriage, yet He had not deserted me. I did not deserve to live, yet He wanted to preserve my life. I did not deserve His love. What fools we are in our despair. We think we know what God should or should not do when all the while He wants to say, "I love you." I could deny my worthiness, but I could not deny the flowers on the wall, nor could I stifle their chorus.

Just to reinforce things, I had a surprise visit from another friend. Somehow, Gail, a good friend from school, had found out I was in the hospital. She had come to visit me. I was ashamed, stunned, embarrassed, and confused. Her compassion and non-judgmental response to my despair surprised me. She was a Christian, yet she accepted me, divorce, frailties, and all. She took me in her arms and whispered through her own tears, "Oh, Carole, God loves you so much." Although I might have tried to negate the flowers on the wall, I could not reject her absolute faith and integrity.

Where had she come from? How did she find me? My hospitalization was supposed to be confidential. How did she happen to show up just at that moment? God had given me the gift of her friendship and the irises at the exact moment when the world had told me God was a cosmic joke. I would stand. I might not ever dance to the music, but as of that day, I would at least think about standing up and going back for more. It absolutely never occurred to me to fight anymore. I was no warrior. The thought never even remotely entered my conscious mind.

The Gulf

Summer passed and soon autumn bells called us back. By fall, we were assigned a new principal and started a new year, but clouds still hovered over the faculty. Dark shadows filled the hallways, and, one by one, people sought refuge in quiet corners of their own rooms or even off campus whenever possible. A few even hid out in the basement where they shared cigarettes and coffee during their prep periods and lunch. A dank mist glued itself to the glass that pretended to illuminate classrooms lucky enough to have windows. Air literally became harder and harder to breathe. Although the spiritual stench was sickening, most didn't understand why they couldn't get enough oxygen. We blamed the ventilation system; we blamed the smog; we blamed the pollen. We worked and waited. When would the next volcano erupt? So much damage had been done, yet I was relieved in a way because these particular vapors had nothing to do with me or my personal life. After all we had been through, most people retreated into their private bunkers. Morning minutes at the mailboxes were "grab and go," and each day more empty chairs appeared in the lunchroom. Yet another new principal now declared herself "The Queen of Orange and Green", our school colors, and did everything she could to make us believe order was restored. She tried so hard to get us to cheer up that some took her joviality and threw it back at her like a pie in the face. Some said, "The sun'll come out tomorrow," but it was too late. The thunder had roared, shaking our foundations, blasting our stability. Absolutely nothing was the same at our high school, and we all knew it. For many, trust had been totally obliterated. One day at the beginning of the term, I shared my Yosemite adventure to a captive audience of new ninth graders. They were incredibly attentive, which I attributed to their intense anxiety level. A few days later, a sweet young lady in my third period class asked if she could talk to me after class. "Sure, honey." I smiled, figuring she had some kind of problem adjusting to high school.

"I need to give you a message," she said shyly. "It's very important. It's private."

"Of course," I responded as I closed the door. "What is it, Sweety?"

"I told your story to my mother, and she shared it with the elders. I hope you aren't mad at me."

"What story? I mean which one? Why would I be mad?" I laughed, not understanding the importance of our conversation, but still trying to be respectful to the shy little blonde girl with the big brown eyes.

"The one you told us about the eagle. My people say it is very important." she said.

"Yes, I think so, too. It was a very significant experience for me. I am glad you liked the story. So, what did your mother say?"

"Well, it's kind of important to my people," she stammered.

"What do you mean?" I looked at her solemn brown eyes and hoped those were not tears I saw welling up.

"I know I don't look it, but I am Cherokee," she murmured. I lifted her head and as our eyes met, I assured her she should be very proud of her heritage.

"Well, anyway, I hope you aren't mad," she very softly repeated.

"How could I possibly be mad at you?" I answered gently.

"Actually, I am very anxious to hear what you have to say. It really is OK. Honestly." My words felt ineffective as I realized I was confronting much more than just a few days worth of anxiety over high school.

"Well, the elders say the eagle came to you from the Great Spirit for a very important reason. You must ask what he wants to tell you. It is a very great sign. Please don't be mad at me." This shy young girl had no idea of how much I wanted to scoop her up and tell her it was all just fine with me. I not only accepted what she had to say but loved her on the spot for a million and one reasons. There was no way I would let her get away without telling her she was confirming what God had tried to tell me.

"So, you're not mad at me?" she asked.

"Not in a million years. Trust me." I begged. She assured me she would trust me. So now I not only had to deal with the fact that the eagle meant something to me personally, I also had to acknowledge that it also meant something to a very special child in my class and her people.

"I promise you I will consider all that you have shared with me, and I will ask God what He has to say." I meant what I said to her. I valued her sincerity. I went home and put off scoring all the diagnostic reading tests until morning. Instead, I scanned all the notes I had collected, trying to figure out what it was that made the eagle so magnificently important to so many different people. I read all the scriptures I could remember about eagles. Repeatedly, I asked God, "What does it all mean? Did it all really happened? Was it real?"

Silence. Then a soft whisper, "I know the plans I have for you. . . plans for welfare and not for evil, to give you a future and a hope" (Jeremiah 29:11). I wasn't exactly sure what He meant to say to me through His word.

It would have been wonderful if God just popped in and yelled, "Hello, it's me!" I get really frustrated with those individuals who say they can ask God a question and get an instamatic answer. Most of the time, He just tells me, "Wait." Waiting is not one of my talents. Meanwhile, the eagle just adjusted his shoulders, glanced my way, and resumed position. I had to go on with the program. I had to score the tests, interpret the data, and teach my classes, ready or not. Each day was a new challenge, but academic challenges are really not as difficult as those dished out by life in the spiritual arena.

To make matters worse, the morning paper signaled another call to arms and suddenly, the world was upside down again. The Gulf War had erupted in the Middle East. Naturally, as an educator, I had known tensions were brewing over there, but like most, I was not paying much attention. Instantly, that changed. Many of our former students had been sent overseas, and some had found a way to come back and say a quick, "Good bye. I love you. Please write." Over the next few weeks, I gave out their addresses to students who might want to send a card or a note and handed out little flags to those who wanted to show support for our friends who were now serving far away in Middle East. One afternoon, I walked into my department chair's room for the regular monthly meeting and heard my former friends declare "Carole probably thinks this war is Armageddon." Snickers punctuated mockery. Everyone laughed riotously.

"And what on earth does she think she is doing with those stupid little flags?" The new temporary art teacher was particularly snide and arrogant. "The sight of that red, white and blue just makes me want to vomit," she added. I could not believe what she said. At that point, I wanted to vomit. Who was she? Where had she come from anyway? We had known some of these soldiers, sailors, marines, and airmen for at least four years. These were our kids, our country, and our flag she was vilifying. What was even more of a personal shock to me was that one of those who joined the mockery was a Vietnam War veteran. I swallowed the bitter taste in my throat and went to her room later that day just to talk and somehow justify my little flags and my strong patriotism without telling her I had heard the conversation at lunch. As I walked into her ceramics class, I realized I had entered a revolting phallic forest of artistic expression. To her and others, "free expression" in America meant they could say or do just whatever they wanted, even if it was disgusting. Checked by the Holy Spirit, I knew I was in enemy territory. She wasn't there at the moment, so I did a pivot and left. I should have been getting used to it all, but I was not. Pretending to be open with my old roommate was another challenge, but I managed to pull it off. I even asked her if she wanted a few little flags. It would have been professional suicide on my part to confront her or or any of them. I actually thought it was just one more consequence God required because I had failed him so miserably. If I couldn't save my marriage or my family, what made me think I could save any friendships?

When I ran into another member of the English Department later that day, she could tell I was upset. Some people are like that. I shared only that I was sad over the war and over the remarks I had heard by some people in our department. "But, Carole, why would you want them in your quality world?" She laughed, gave me a hug and took at least a dozen flags for her students. "Hang in there. Lots of people love you. We all need to support our troops and their families." She was right about that. I smiled, but I was really hurting inside.

Of course, I had other friends whom I dearly loved.

My childhood friend, Donna, had written to me with words of love and comfort, telling me that if God had not healed my marriage, He had a very good reason. In fact, she would have been willing to tell me quite a few of those reasons; however, she had been wonderfully kind and wise to say nothing along those lines at that time. Instead, she sent encouragement and compassion. We wrote and called each other, sharing the frustrations we encountered, not only as teachers, but as Christian teachers in a hostile world. Donna and I had been friends since junior high school, and there was little we did not know and accept about one another. In a long, interesting lifetime of coincidences, we had shared everything from the births of our children to

The Gulf

the fulfillment of our dreams to become teachers. As it ended up, I was at the high school level, and she was teaching first grade. What neither of us had been ready for was the assault on our values and our faith in Jesus Christ. That evening, she called me from far away. Without knowing about my terrible day, my friend had reached out, not just to tell me she loved me, but to say clearly, "God loves you, no matter what, and so do I." I wanted to believe her. No matter how many people God sent to tell me He loved me, I was dead sure He did not. I wanted to run, but this time there was nowhere to run, nowhere to hide. I certainly did not have the will to fight. I certainly did not have the strength. What she didn't tell me during our conversation was that she had sent me a beautiful print of a single iris in full bloom. It arrived the next afternoon. God's flower soothed my contentious spirit, and I truly was comforted.

Nevertheless, the snide remarks from those former close friends and new colleagues were just the beginning of the next wave. At first, our principal tried to be positive and upbeat. She had lots of quirks, but most of them made us often laugh at her. Nevertheless, rumbling continued as legislators complained about money and a million other things. Our district, like so many, was in another one of those budget deficit crunches. I didn't know all the details, and in my confusion, I never dared to ask about specifics. If I had asked, I would have immediately discovered that one financial crisis or another tends to hit every ten years or so. Someday, someone will figure out what causes it and blow their cover, but in the meantime, politicians play cruel games with people, putting one in the side pocket and another behind the eight ball. They cover it all up with euphemisms like "cutting back," "downsizing", or "surplusing." No matter what anyone calls it, it hurts. This time I was on the list and was told I would not be returning to Mesa Verde in the fall. My former "friend" told me our department chair liked someone else better. I was crushed, especially when I realized I had more seniority and was better qualified than the person chosen to stay in my place. I had entwined my heart into the fabric of our small community, but it was over. At least that is what I was told, and I believed it. I was determined to keep myself together. There would be no tears to turn into transgressions. I would keep my head and my heart under control.

Even as I began to empty my classroom, other people came to say, "Don't give up. This isn't right. These things happen in education. Besides, you have seniority, and you're a great teacher." I knew they meant well; I even hoped they were right. Even so, if the new principal had added my name to the surplus list, I must have done something wrong. I realized it was often more about politics than actual professionalism. I also figured God was disgusted with me, and I was getting what I deserved. I packed everything and emptied my classroom, once again trying to second guess God. After all, since I had failed Him, it made perfect sense that He would take away the job He had given me as a birthday present years before. I was "guilty as charged" and deserved what I got. I paid very little attention to all the wonderful people who came by and told me to stand up for myself. I was not in any mood to stand up for myself. I was not a warrior, not in my own eyes. At least this time when I cried, I shut the door. I wasn't the only one being treated unfairly. Interestingly, I had no trouble telling others to stand up for themselves. Injustice aggravated me when it concerned other people. My dear friend Gail's name was also on the list, and she had done nothing to deserve it. She, too, was a devout Christian, someone those snide critics liked to call the "Church Lady". Her crimes? Christianity. Kindness. Compassion. Ethics. Unashamed faith. Though I was certain God was not about to help me, I was certain He would help my friend. She was an incredibly good person. This just was not fair. Gail and I sat in the quiet corner of my room and softly asked God to tell us what to do, yet fighting for our rights was farthest from our mind at that point. As we prayed, Gail said things were going to be OK. I thought that meant we would get other jobs. She went to another friend who just happened to be a Christian and told her our situation. Her sister in Christ did not like what she heard and told Gail the situation was not only unacceptable, but illegal. Of course, I did not have a clue about any of this. Gail did, and so did her friend. As an administrator, the friend went to our principal and set her straight. I had no idea anything, was going on at the time.

Soon it was time for the Junior Prom and Senior Ball, and like I had always done, I attended, delighting in the beautiful gowns and handsome couples that filled the dance floor. This year, the celebration was held on an old riverboat that cruised the river in the moonlight. One of the parents who volunteered to chaperone was a very delightful lady whose personality endeared her to the kids and faculty alike. That night, she kept telling the story of how she had tipped over a canoe as a child and thought she was going to drown in the lake. He brother, knowing the lake was only a few feet deep, kept telling her. "Stand up, stupid! Stand up!" The lady kept telling the story all night, and, ironically, I would just happen to be standing beside her every time she did. Of course, in my own mind, all I kept thinking was that this would be my last Senior Ball, and I would miss these kids very much. I was lost in thought, wondering about the layoffs, the uncertainty, and the utter unfairness of it, trying to figure out what God wanted me to do. "What should I do, God?" I asked. "How can I know what you want of me?"

"Stand up, stupid!" This time she was practically yelling in my ear. "Stand up!" Oh! Somewhere in my heart, something awakened. "Having done all, stand." (Ephesians 6:13). Suddenly, I recognized His voice. I did not have to fight this battle. It was not my fight. If God wanted Gail and me to go or to stay, we would do whatever He commanded. For now, He was telling us to stand. That's all. Just stand. "You will not need to fight in this battle; take your position; stand still, and see the victory of the Lord in your behalf" (2 Chronicles 20:17). 1 wanted to run and tell Gail the minute I got to school, but I was just too afraid. Amazingly, I questioned whether or not it was really God's voice I had heard on the water that night, and was afraid I might be reading something into nothing. I feared she would think I was trying to be something I wasn't. I was just generally insecure, terrified to be exact.

"Who do you think you are?" My mother's voice echoed in my soul. "Why would God talk to the likes of you?" While I battled with doubts and despair, I prepared for the potluck we were supposed to have at our English Department meeting. I decided I would talk to Gail later. As she and I walked into the room, we heard our "friends" and colleagues sarcastically singing, "Amazing Grace, how sweet the sound," followed by snickers and soft laughter. I turned to leave just as Gail came through the door. "Stand!" God whispered. I held back my tears, hoping she had not heard their mockery. I was angry. How dare they attack her? It was too late. She had heard it all. It was one thing for me to fail my Lord. In a twisted way, I still figured I deserved to be mocked. It was quite another to sit there and listen to my friend being ridiculed. I got rip roaring mad.

It would be much more professional to say I chose to allow the two atheists and their friends to openly express alternative views. Indeed, everyone does have a right to freely express an opinion, and most of the time I can just shrug it off. That day was different. First of all, the song was initiated in contempt. Moreover, a few professed Christians had joined with confirmed atheists in cruel mockery of a precious child of God. Gail had done nothing wrong and was no threat to any of them. I am ashamed to admit that out of sheer cowardice I stood there and kept my mealy mouth shut. I hated myself that night. In the quiet darkness, the eagle ruffled its feathers, turned its head and stretched itself in readiness.

The next day, Gail came to see how I was, not even concerned for herself. Later, I finally told her how angry I was at the way they mocked her behind her back and what they had done. She just hid under a rock and said, "That's just how it is." Nevertheless, I knew it was just not right. The eagle was on alert. I didn't know it then, but Gail had already found the courage to stand and see what God would do. God also wanted me to stand. God had much more to say to me. Gail came to see me the next day, ready to offer words of comfort in our despair. Her whole focus seemed to be on how I felt. My whole focus was suddenly on the injustice of her treatment. We both were to be surplused. "Fine" I told God. "They don't like me anyway, but as for Gail, Lord it's not fair!"

"I like you just fine. I love all my kids. Both of you are important to me." He said. I bumped into Gail after school, and her encouraging attitude lifted my spirits. "How are you doing?" I asked.

"I'm fine," she replied. "How are you doing?" Of course. What else would she say? She trusted God in all things. I no longer trusted anyone. We decided to pray. God said, "Stand." Sheepishly, I shared His words with Gail. We talked about the battle of Jericho and how Joshua had been commanded to march around the city with his men. Interestingly, that had been the focal point of the sermon in church last week and the week before. God likes to make sure He gets through. I told Gail I had the weird idea that God was telling me to walk around the school, claiming it for Him. "I think He is telling us to march," I said, "to stand and see His victory in our behalf." I was certain He wanted to protect and defend her. It made perfect sense. The previous year, I had I started to walk on a regular basis; often I would run the track. Sometimes in frustration I would run it seven or eight times. To see us walking would not be thought unusual. On this day, Gail and I marched the perimeter of our school seven times.

Although we both knew what we were doing, her faith was absolute. Mine was feeble. We asked God to help us, help our friends, and help our school. Since the district was reshuffling personnel, we even dared to ask God to send more Christians to our campus, not to proselytize, but just to reinforce honesty and decent values. We knew all about separation of church and state. Whether it was students, teachers, administrators, office clerks or custodians, we needed reinforcements. We did not ask for personal favors. We accepted the fact that God could do whatever He decided to do with our lives. On the other hand, God was telling us to claim this territory for Him. We pledged our loyalty and our love to Him. I was still angry that God would allow my friend to be treated with such disrespect and disdain. I wanted to punch somebody's lights out. God said, "Just stand."

Almost daily after school, we talked and prayed. In reality, Gail's faith held me together. I wanted to run as far away from those people as I could get. I did not want to be where I was not wanted. It was Gail who reminded me it was not really their decision. Whether or not we stayed at that school was God's decision. It wasn't even the principal's decision. We walked. We waited. We wondered what He would do. I was grateful for Gail's kindness, yet felt I was unworthy of her friendship. I was such a failure. She never wavered, never accepted my twisted logic. Over several afternoons, many people came by to tell me I should stand up for myself. I just smiled, thanking them all for their kindness. Then I got a note from the principal asking me to come to her office. I did not want to go. I mustered up all the courage I could and plastered a phony smile. Sitting in her office, I listened to her explain all the reasons for the surplusing of teachers and the very dire economic situation of our district. Then, matter of factly, she smiled and said, "You're staying. So is Gail." I felt like someone had plugged me into an electrical outlet. I asked no questions. "Thank you so much" is all that came out of my mouth and my heart. At that point, I didn't know another administrator had told our principal it would be illegal to surplus either one of us. I was stunned by the principal's announcement. Nevertheless, I was all too aware of the complexity and deceit within the English Department and the malicious delight with which some people devoured others.

At the same time, I was ecstatic! Amazing grace, indeed! Let them eat the cake of their craft. God's grace is indeed amazing. Gail's courage was validated beyond anyone's wildest dreams, yet she told absolutely no one, not even me, that she had stood while I whimpered in despair. She was strong while I was wallowing in the mud of shame, self-pity, and failure. Years passed before she ever shared the fact that she had stood in the gap for us, and God had rescued us both. She had never believed I was a failure, neither in her eyes or God's. As for me, I was just stunned. I knew the others in my department would be angry and lay as many booby traps as possible before the semester ended. I just wanted to run. We all finished the year with dignity and feigned friendship. For me, that was indeed a remarkable triumph. With a childhood like mine, the natural thing would have been to get bitter and seek retribution. Instead, I just decided to trust God and start over. I carried all those boxes of my materials and books back to school and set up my classroom all over again. I didn't know what God was thinking, but it didn't matter. I truly believed He had acted in our behalf, and I was truly grateful. Again, the eagle turned, looked, watched, and waited.

Into the Wilderness

Although the immediate crisis was over, my principal complicated everything by asking me to become the English Department Chair. I thanked her politely, and I respectfully declined. I wasn't even sure I wanted to stay at the school, but I kept that to myself. At that point, I still wanted to run away, relocate, and rebuild my life. I had always felt more centered and closer to God when I was out of the frenzy of cities and sirens, so I decided to look for a house in the foothills. After looking at dozens homes and acreage, I finally found a fourteen acre parcel in the mountains. It was a beautiful spot filled with tall pines, manzanita, and yellow scotch broom. To make it even better, a natural spring bubbled near the top of the property and spilled into a clear-running creek where deer and raccoons came to drink and browsed on lush blackberry bushes. At the time, I didn't care that it was sixty miles from my job because I had heard the school district up there needed high school teachers.

When I accidentally stumbled onto a model log cabin displayed beside the freeway, it was as if a lifetime dream was coming into focus. As a child, and for much of my adult life, I had doodled in the margins as I took notes during long, boring classes, lectures, or meetings. Over and over again, I would draw a little log cabin in the pines, with rocks forming the bottom story and chimney that launched soft clouds into the winter sky. Perhaps, I should have known better, but building my own log cabin in the mountains seemed like a perfect idea at the time. I prayed about it before I signed the papers. I made inquiries at the Better Business Bureau and checked everything out quite thoroughly. I did not rush into my adventure lightly, but responsibly. I had no doubt in my mind that the Lord was, indeed, preparing a place for me in the wilderness, and I was not afraid. Finally, I thought I had God and my future all figured out. I would build the cabin, get a new job, and start my life all over again under my own conditions. While He truly was separating me, calling me to be apart from the world to rely upon Him completely, it was all going to be on His conditions.

At first, the project started out quite well. I climbed to the highest point on the property and selected a site close enough to the top to be accessible for the equipment. I rearranged the floor plan of the model I had seen. I had the plans drawn up, a building account set up at the bank, and construction was soon underway. The bank officer had warned me to be very careful not to pay for one thing until it was completed and to read everything very carefully. He had some serious misgivings about a single woman building any house on her own, let alone a log cabin way out in the mountains. His advice turned out to be invaluable. It wasn't long before the people who were supposed to help me coordinate everything tipped their hands. Constant delays, complications, and outright shenanigans kept me on my toes every waking moment. I watched every penny, read every word on every piece of paper, and attended every inspection. As it turned out, I was much luckier than most of the other people who had contracted with the log home company. That is another story waiting to be told. When it all came to a screeching halt, several people had lost a great deal of money. Tragically, one family had been bilked out of $80,000. It is hard to imagine how that could happen, but the world is filled with con artists, dishonest people, and outright crooks. I was lucky. I had God coaching me through every crisis, telling me what to do and how to do it. More and more, I was learning to rely solely upon Him.

After almost a year of hassles, I moved into my beautiful log cabin in the pines. My front door faced the bright morning sun. From the deck outside my kitchen on the opposite side of the house, I could see forever as I watched that sun slip into the shadows at twilight. Evenings, I was serenaded by what must have been a million frogs singing under a blanket of stars. Never had I seen so many stars. Listening to the music of the night, I would lie on my deck "catch the falling stars, put them in my pocket, save them for a rainy day". Never had I felt such glorious peace. Indeed, I did "go out in joy, led forth in peace, the mountains and the hills before [me] broke forth into singing, and all the trees of the field [did]clap their hands"(Isaiah 55:12).

Weekends, I set to work cleaning up the huge construction mess. I had thought the builders would do all that, but they had a bigger disaster to deal with as they battled angry clients and attorneys. Since there was no hope of getting a hand from anyone else, at least not without spending a tremendous amount of money, I got to work. I burned what trash I could and made a big pile of materials to dump. Then I started clearing a section where I would keep the horses I planned to buy. After my third bout with poison oak, I took a neighbor's advice and bought a small pigmy goat. She was an adorable silver and black doe that was literally in goat heaven as she nibbled on leaves, scotch broom, manzanita, poison oak, and my flowers. Whoops! Goats eat everything. Right away, I bought some portable fencing and sectioned out an area where I thought she would be happy for quite a while. I even constructed a small shelter for her from leftover scraps of wood. I nailed pieces of lumber onto the sides of old sawhorses and patted myself on the back for my ingenuity. The little hut I made was just the exactly correct size for one little goat.

The next morning, I went out to feed her and literally squealed with amazement. My daughter had driven out to visit and came racing out of the house to see what in the world was wrong. Nothing was wrong. To my complete surprise, my little silver doe had given birth to little black twins in the middle of the night. The tiny little bucks were the cutest things I had ever seen, and our hearts exploded with laughter as we watched them bounce across the leaves. Boing! Boing! Needless to say, it wasn't long before I built more little huts, and moved the portable fencing. Meanwhile, I took a few lessons to get ready for the day I would buy my first horse. I knew very little about horses except for the fact that I loved them. The first time I saw Star, I fell in love with the little black and white pinto, wrote a check, and arranged to bring her home. She and the goats, which by now numbered half a dozen, were my new family, and building my place in the mountains filled every spare moment. When my sister Susie, who lived in Georgia, found out I had actually bought a horse, she could not contain her excitement. When I opened the card she sent to express her delight, hundreds of tiny, sparkling, shimmering stars exploded like the Fourth of July. Next, I bought chickens to eat the bugs and my cats kept the snakes and mice in their place.

One night, I heard a frightening screech echoing in the darkness and raced out onto my deck to see what was happening. There in the curved arm of an old oak tree that sheltered the goat pen, a golden mountain lion sat ready to pounce. I yelled for Gabe, my Great Pyrannees. I had bought my fluffy white puppy just after I broke ground on the property, and he was about a year old now. I had counted on him to be my faithful companion and fearless guardian. Gabe came bounding out onto the deck to save us all. He took one look over the railing and froze. With a hearty, "Woof!" and a high pitched, "Yelp!" he dashed back inside, flew into the bedroom, and scrunched his eighty pound body under the bed. "Some guard dog," I laughed. In a flash, I turned on every light in the house, the television, and the radio. I grabbed the biggest pots I could and ran out onto the deck yelling at the top of my lungs, "Get out of here! What do you think you're doing?" In an instant, the big hungry cat turned, looked at me, and took off. "And stay out!" I hollered. When things settled down, I crawled under the bed to tell Gabe the coast was clear, ruffled his furry neck, and laughed myself to sleep. I was also praising God in gratitude.

The next day at the feed store I soon learned mountain lions were not the only creatures that stalked the shadows in Garden Valley. Forest fires and increased building in the hills had forced many bears to move closer to town, and they were very often discovered in someone's garage or backyard. Truly, the Lord had brought me into the wilderness. Although many people thought I was a little crazy for living so far out, I had little time to be lonely or afraid. My heart was filled with gratitude. Although I didn't' notice it, as I faced each new challenge, I was growing physically, emotionally, and spiritually stronger. The next summer, I decided to look for a teaching position closer to my new home. A lady at the church I had begun to attend confirmed that the district was indeed looking for teachers, so I felt pretty confident when I picked up the paperwork. When I looked at the pay scale, however, my bubble popped. I would have to take a $14,000 a year in salary if I changed jobs. I put the papers in a drawer and thought about nothing else for weeks. August came, and it was time to start a new semester. I weighed my options as I followed muddy pickups and logging trucks through the narrow road that stretched across the valley and twisted through the winding canyon. I thought about it every time a big SUV cut me off on the freeway each morning or whenever I was stuck in afternoon traffic heading home. One evening, as I fed Star and listened to the goats argue and boss each other around, I came to the conclusion that the many rewards of living so close to nature made the long drive worth it all. I would handle the beasts in the wild, the beasts on the road, and the beasts at school. God had brought me to this place, and I was prepared to stay forever. That weekend when I stopped to buy my groceries, He had yet another surprise. The market was giving away free china with every ten dollars spent on groceries. Beautiful blue irises decorated the center and rim of every plate, bowl, cup, and saucer. Week by week, I collected all the pieces, gravy boat, platters and all. My broken dishes had been replaced, one by one. Truly, the Lord had "prepared a table before me in the presence of mine enemies. . .My cup runneth over." (Psalm 23:6.). God was really going out of His way to show His love for me.

Along with a commitment to stay at my school came a commitment to do my very best for my students and to honor my own integrity by keeping my mouth shut. Sharing my personal heartaches and Christian values had brought me extra discomfort. I vowed to do my job, period. I was not going to get attached to students, worry about their safety, or lose sleep when they didn't pass their classes. Furthermore, I was not going to talk about God or discuss my spiritual growth. I had been dumb enough to expose myself to ridicule, deception, and betrayal, but I was not going to do that ever again. Ha!

First of all, I couldn't even get up in the morning without God, let alone face so many other challenges. I was not a morning person, but my rooster crowed at 4:00 a.m. whether I was ready or not. Getting to school wasn't that bad because I could listen to Christian tapes or the radio while I played tag with the trucks. I practiced being "professionally aloof" for awhile, but eventually my heart kicked my head. I am not ruled by logic. I was careful, however, about sharing any secrets, secrets like, "God is so cool! The irises are blooming, and they don't even know it is the wrong time of year!" By now, my little goat community had grown to over a dozen. They shared the pen with Star, my horse, fourteen Arucana chickens, and two peacocks. Together they cleared the land of poison oak, ate the bugs, and gave me fresh eggs every morning. Every once in a while, one of the little pygmy goats would get out of the pen, and I would chase after it, shooing it to safety. One night as I drove up driveway my headlights caught little twin babies romping across the road. It was dark, it was cold, and I was tired. I got out of the car and managed to get one inside the gate. The other was having a good time of tag with me. Finally getting him near the pen, I stopped suddenly and looked right into the eyes of a beautiful deer.

The gentle female looked straight at me, stared for a moment, and stepped out of the shadows towards the pen. She looked at the baby goat and bent down, gently nudging his rump. Instantly, the cocky little kid dashed inside the gate. The doe stepped back, looked straight into my eyes, and quickly hopped far back into the brush before I could say, "Thank you, mam." It was amazing, absolutely amazing. I liked this place!

My interactions with the animals brought much joy, encouragement, and inspiration. Every little sub culture had a set of rules and expectations for each other. The goats especially would discipline one another with a "Whup! Whup! Whup!" and openly argue over who had what rights to food or the little huts. They needed more space, so I decided to build a small stable in which the goats, the horse, the chickens, and two peacocks could safely spend the chilly nights. After lots of looking, I finally found a young man who agreed to do the work for a reasonable fee. He came out, framed the shelter, and said he would be back in the morning. I never saw him again. Great! Now what would I do? Where was I going to find another inexpensive replacement? I picked up a hammer, some nails, a few boards and went to work. "I'm no carpenter," I wailed every time I smashed a finger.

"I am," a soft voice inside answered. Between the two of us, Jesus and I built a small, barn. Can you believe it? Everyone was so happy with it that not even one goat complained about whose spot was whose, even when the cats came to check it out. We were all ready for the winter, and not a minute too soon. Icy winds brought power outages, snowstorms, and freezing temperatures which coated the mountain roads with black ice. Sometimes I couldn't even get out of my driveway. Heavy rains caused massive flooding, trees fell, and roads were often closed. Weird as it may sound, it never occurred to me to be afraid. Indeed, God had given "His angels charge over [me] to guard [me] in all [my] ways " (Psalms 91:11).

Awakenings

I often shared my little stories with Gail and wrote to my friend Donna often to reassure her I was safe and sound. Sometimes I brought irises to school and put them on my desk. Sometimes I brought some for Gail, too. Then one day she shared how worried she was about her son. Eric had a very serious sinus infection that required a surgical process. It required the surgeon to cut extremely close to sensitive nerves. A slip could mean permanent brain damage. Naturally, she was very anxious about the whole process, but she didn't share her worst fears with her son. We prayed about it, asking God to keep a special eye on her Eric and to help the doctors as they worked on him. Gail told me that her fears were swept aside when she saw a beautiful picture of an iris over her son's bed. Because I had shared my story about the iris as part of God's precious love and faithfulness to me, she recognized the fact that He had sent the iris as a sign of His faithfulness in all things especially for her. She told me she knew from the instant she saw the iris, that all would be well, not because of a flower on the wall, but because of God. Flowers don't make miracles, but God does it all the time. How natural it is for Him to send flowers to His beloved children.

A few years before, I had also shared my story about the iris at one of our Senior Girl's lunches. At the time, it was a perfectly natural thing to do, and the girls loved it. I never thought much about it afterwards and, in fact, I probably never would, but something interesting and unusual came out one day as I stopped to talk to my friend Vivian. Vivian's daughter, Rosie, had married her high school sweetheart, Bob, who had also been one of my favorite students. Bob was a wonderful young man whose greatest fault was telling me to close my eyes and not worry so much about my students. I didn't listen to him that afternoon in the hallway, but I did listen to him another day when it was his own heart that was on the rack. I had listened to Rosie, too, on a cold winter afternoon as she poured out her personal pain. I remember sharing how things can look so bleak, so dark, and so disastrous when they are covered in the mud of circumstance, yet under the mud, a flower is getting ready to be born. It was my conversation with her that prompted me to share it with the other girls at our weekly lunches.

As young people get ready to graduate from high school, a myriad of emotions emerge, often causing heartache, confusion, and despair. While many are excited about graduation, others are often terrified and insecure at the same time. Arguments with parents are frequent, and best friends break up over silly things. If we can help them see beyond the rain of sorrows, seeds of hope have a fighting chance. Rosie waded through the mud and found her feet again. So did Bob. Their paths merged into one, and, although many said they were too young, they decided to marry. As a wedding present, I gave them a pewter light switch plate depicting an iris. Since Bob had enlisted in the United States Air Force, it wasn't long until they were sent to Alaska. Alaska! Rosie would have followed Bobby to the ends of the earth, and she did just that. She went to Alaska. She had no friends waiting to welcome her, but the Lord had a very special surprise. He gave her living, precious friend, a young lady named Iris. We both got the message.

Soon after that, I had a junior class for the outer realm. These kids did not really like school, at least not the academic side of it. Many of them were cheerleaders and athletes, so their minds were always on the next game. The only trouble was, I knew too much about what happened after the games. I fought my urge to get involved with every ounce of my intellect. Part of me didn't want to know. I didn't want to care so much. When some of the football players came to class bleary eyed, I knew it wasn't from the heat of practice. When I sent them to the office, nothing ever happened. If I told them I was worried, they just shrugged it off, laughing and hugging me on their way out the door. One day, I shut the door and let them all have it. I said it was fine if they wanted to fake out the rest of the people on campus, but they were scaring me. I told them about all the things I had heard, holding back every tear that screamed behind my eyes. "Please," I begged. "Stop this behavior before someone is dead. I don't want to go to anyone's funeral. "You really don't know what you are doing."

"Ms B, you worry too much. We love you."

"We're not stupid. We're the smart kids."

"Thanks, Ms B, but we really are OK, honest."

Yep, I had heard all that before. In time, every one of them graduated. Some moved away, and others went off to college on athletic scholarships. Maybe I had worried too much after all. Maybe I was just a bit melodramatic. That would be me, of course, always seeing beyond the concrete things in front of my face. "Just deal with the facts, Carole," I told myself. "You really do worry too much." One morning, scanning the newspaper as usual, I noticed the headline on an article on one of the back pages. My heart did a painful flip. I read the article over and over. Dustin was dead. He had been murdered and dumped in a ditch. Not Dustin. Not my Dustin. Yes, my sweet, gentle Dustin. Our Dustin .Everybody's Dustin. I wanted to scream, but nothing came out. I just picked up my papers and went to school. Yes, it was true, all true. The funeral would be in a few days. Of course, I went. Of course, it was harder than I ever expected. I hadn't buried any of my students yet, but that wasn't the worst part. The worst of it was seeing so many precious kids decimated by grief, their hearts ground into the reality that their dear friend was gone. The really hard part was looking into one boy's eyes as he said, "It didn't have to happen, Ms B. It didn't have to happen. Why didn't we listen to you? Why?"

"We all loved him so much," I stumbled for words, cradling him in my arms for a moment. As I looked around the church at the pictures and the flowers, my eyes fell on a beautiful bouquet of purple iris, tied with a ribbon and a note, "We love you, Dustin."

Things like that began to pop out at the least expected moment. As they did, I thought maybe I wasn't supposed to keep my mouth totally shut. Maybe I should even share my story. "Of course, you have to," Gail insisted. Donna insisted, too.

"I guess," I smiled, still not too sure. Then my friend Janice shared that she had been diagnosed with advanced breast cancer . The news was so devastating that I was lost for words of comfort or encouragement. Janice had said she wasn't a Christian. In fact, she wasn't sure what she believed. I told her the story of the iris and wanted to leave it at that. I gave her an iris plant and a few things with irises on them, trying just to say, "God and I love you very much." A real fighter, she actually wrote a grant to get her insurance company to allow a complete bone marrow transplant and began chemotherapy with all it entailed. As Gail and I prayed, she said she just knew Janice would come through everything well. She was right. Soon, the cancer was in remission, and Janice laughed when her hair came back in very curly. We all rejoiced, and while I praised God for His mercy, I forgot all about the iris story. I didn't know whether it had meant anything to her one way or the other. The next year, Janice came back to school and took up where she left off. One day, I noticed she was wearing a blouse that was almost covered with many purple irises. She never said a word. I never said a word. " Hey, God, look," I whispered one day as I realized she was wearing it again. God smiled. Me, too

Commissioned

*B*y then I was pretty much back on track emotionally, and so was my teaching. One day the principal left a note in my mailbox asking me to stop in and see her before I went home. I popped my head into her office that afternoon, and she said the district office had called to ask if I would send some samples of my work in a little portfolio. She didn't really know what they wanted, but told me to call down there and clarify if I was agreeable. "Sure," I smiled. I was used to sharing things with other teachers and assumed it was part of our district's writing specialist program. I called, connected with a secretary, and was asked to represent the district along with many of my colleagues from other schools. We were all asked to attend a meeting at the county office to talk about strategies and activities we found successful when working with adolescents. When I arrived, I signed in, smiled at my friends, and found an empty seat. The room was packed with teachers from several districts, and many were people I recognized as talented and dedicated educators.

What neither I nor anyone else that day was that we were being called to muster that cold gray October afternoon. Most of us already realized we were "engaged in a great Civil War" a battle for every child, every parent, every person in our communities. We were all dedicated professionals, determined to reach and to teach our children, to help them learn, to help them learn, to help them survive. Here in California, where so many different cultures collide, none of us had the luxury of spare time. Nevertheless, the National Board for Professional Teaching Standards was officially sounding the trumpet. None of us knew or understood what it was we were being asked to do. The man at the podium told us the country was at risk and we were being called to active duty. All across the nation kids were in crisis. Were we willing to help? The man and his assistants passed out a few forms and gave us a brief, very brief explanation of something called a certification process. We were all invited to create a small portfolio of successful teaching strategies to share with other educators across the country. At first, it seemed a little inconvenient considering that Homecoming, WASC reports, and the holidays were on the horizon. Nevertheless, I signed my name at the bottom of a list and was told I would get more information in the mail.

A short time later, the box landed like a bomb, boldly scattering a colorful collection of booklets across my family room floor. Each booklet focused on a particular section of the portfolio which was to be completed by early January. January? It was already November. By definition, portfolio assessment involves analysis, organization, interpretation, explanation, synthesis, evaluation, and communication allowing for variety. This is what we expect from our students, but we guide our learners with clear directions and help them along the way as they prepare portfolios. All of a sudden, I was asked to create my own portfolio which did all of those things and then some without any clear directions or a nickel's worth of guidance. The portfolio requested involved the completion of several packets, and each packet was expected to meet quite a number of very rigorous standards which were incredibly vague, even for English teachers.

The first packet was relatively simple because it asked for my professional background and evidence of partnership with the educational community. Writing and developing the Careers in Education program over several years had already created a unique partnership with elementary schools and daycare centers in the community. For that reason, completion of the first section was relatively smooth. However, there was no time to waste, no time to ponder over the next section which required detailed, minute by minute documentation of teaching and planning for an uninterrupted, three week period. While good planning is part of every teacher's portfolio, finding time to write a thorough analysis and evaluation of a lesson, reflect upon student involvement, and identify several individual needs was incredibly difficult. I wrote it all down, looked at student performance, and did my best. When I called a friend to ask how we were to do this particular portion of the portfolio, she said, "Are you nuts? I don't have time for that stuff. You aren't getting paid, you know. Don't do it !" I hung up, sighed, and stomped around the house for awhile before feeding the horse, the dogs, the cats, the chickens, and the goats, including the little ones that had just been born. "What am I doing, God?'I muttered as I closed up the corral. "Raising kids," He snickered.

I went back to my dining room table and reviewed my papers, focusing on a few I decided to follow. I wrote everything down in detail and did my best to type it all up, submitting student artifacts as evidence. Night after night, I stayed up to get the sections together. The worst one was the request for unedited videotapes accompanied by an analysis of my lessons. Yuck! I decided to tape part of my freshman autobiographical project which went right along with the papers I was submitting as evidence of student growth. Then, they also wanted us to send a tape of something connected to literature, so I asked a student to film the trial scene I had written to go along with Jack London's *Call of the Wild* The "court" was asked to decide whether or not the dog Buck should be destroyed. On the day I selected for that videotaping, it poured. Forrest was supposed to tape the entire class session, including students entering the room. Yikes! The girls were insistent that they would not be taped with stringy hair, and the boys were teasing them about being "big stars." It could have been a disaster. I told Forrest I could only send one tape. No editing was allowed, and I would love him forever if he would be in charge. He was an angel. I don't know how the thing came out as well as it did. I scanned it. No, I watched it a dozen times, cried, prayed, and sent it. The directions said, "No editing," and I followed the directions. We actually received so few directions that I was afraid to flinch. Completion of all the written work was grueling and at times very confusing. Naturally, release time was out of the question, so I did much of it at night, or in the wee hours of the morning. I groaned. Exhausted, I finally attempted to decipher labeling instructions, packaged my product, and sent the portfolio off in early January. Only a few of my friends had followed through with the ordeal. Like weary soldiers, we were grateful we had survived. We were totally unaware of what was still ahead. One afternoon a few weeks later, a package arrived with a list of novels to be read by the end of March. After all I had already been through, reading a few books was no problem, especially since I was already familiar with most of them. I quickly read all the novels and drove to Rancho Cordova early one wild Saturday morning. March had come in like a lion, and it was snowing in the foothills when I left that morning. I ignored the thunderheads when as they rumbled "Warning! Warning! Stay home!" After all, a relaxed discussion of young adult fiction with congenial colleagues might even be fun. When I splashed across the parking lot and into the library at the school where I had been sent, I smiled at the nice lady and gratefully accepted the warm coffee she offered. Then she outlined the next two days

Iris in the Snow

She explained that we were all to be videotaped as we met, and told us the essay examinations would begin in half an hour. I had driven over the rivers and through the woods, totally unprepared for two solid days of testing in the trenches. Only one very small segment on Sunday afternoon would even deal with the novels we had been asked to read. Essay examinations? What was she saying?

"Did you know we were going to write essays?" one of the ladies asked.

"Are you kidding?" I can't even write my name when I am under pressure," I replied. We were tense.

"We've had it," someone said.

"Now we know how the kids feel," I laughed, trying to joke about the whole thing. Underneath, it just wasn't funny. This was a real test, with real questions, real essays, and real consequences; however, not one of us had any notion of just what those consequences were at the time. We were scared. Well, I was scared. One lady said, "Hey, I'm very good. I'm not concerned at all." Later on my friend and I remembered her comment and laughed. We were very concerned. We were downright worried. We had put an awful lot of ourselves into completing the packets. We had indeed come too far to turn back now. We wrote our essays, graded student papers, wrote our comments, and discussed books while videotapes whirred. We worked very hard well into late afternoon. It was getting dark when we said our final "Good-byes" and "Good lucks" and finally headed for home. As I pulled up into the long driveway, my headlights flashed on the little white patches along the road. There in the darkness, I saw it. Yes. An iris was blooming in the snow.

Completion of the certification process as it was set forth by the National Board for Professional Teaching Standards was a rigorous period of intense self-evaluation and unbelievable stress. Without guidance or support, we had navigated the rapids of reform and met the challenge of change and incredible scrutiny. Like good recruits, we had hurried to the front and fought a good fight. We had heard a rustling in the bushes, aimed, and fired. Did we hit the target? We had no idea. We had submitted samples of our lessons and offered ourselves as sacrifice without even knowing what anyone out there wanted or why we were doing it. Now, we waited. We waited almost two years. We wondered. We waited some more. We worried.

"Have you heard anything? " Gail asked.

"Nothing," I muttered. "I probably blew it."

"You're going to make it," she smiled. "You'll see."

Another graduation came and went. Now another summer promised respite. July boiled over into August. One afternoon, a yellow slip that had been baking in the mailbox said a package from San Antonio was waiting for me. San Antonio was where I had sent my portfolio. "They're sending it back," I thought. Picking up the package was no problem as the local UPS depot was very close to my home. Opening it was quite another matter. "What if ? " I kept asking myself. I kept myself worked up with "What ifs?" for an hour before I finally called the depot and asked the man for directions, so I could drive over and pickup my very important package. I told him it was very important. He told me they were about to close, but he would wait for me. I dashed to beat the clock. When I got there, the nice man handed me a small envelope, not a package. I signed for it, thanked him, and stood there. "Aren't you going to open it?" he asked.

"When I get home," I smiled. I drove down the street and around the comer, thinking I would truly open the envelope when I was safely inside the house. However, I couldn't stand it. I pulled over to the side of the road and peeled open the envelope. As I read the first word, "Congratulations", my heart lept up into my throat and strangled me with awe. I was one of those elite who had been certified as Early Adolescent /Language Arts Specialists. Moreover, I was invited to meet the President of the United States at a special reception in Washington, DC. I was totally afraid to call anyone to ask who else might have made it. Rubrics provided a detailed explanation of the scoring process, and for the first time the target was clarified. Indeed, we had shot from the hip at a bush rustling in the darkness and made a hit. The information helped us determine our individual strengths and validated our innermost beliefs, beliefs about ourselves, beliefs about our teaching, and, most of all, beliefs about our students. As we prepared to go back out there to begin another brand new school year, we were about to straighten our aim. We were going back with new confidence and courage. We were sharing what we had learned because we believed in the integrity of our profession and the teachers of tomorrow.

Keenly aware of how many wonderful teachers work every bit as hard as I do, I was reluctant to share my success. I still really didn't believe I was invited to Washington DC to meet the President of the United States. It was just unreal. At a workshop just before school started, one of the other candidates stood up and proudly announced she was one of only three teachers in our district who had made it. Everybody clapped. Then Gail stood up (which she never does) and said, "And here is another one," pointing to me. People clapped some more; then it was announced that we were actually going to Washington, DC. Yes, we really were going to meet President Bill Clinton.

Oh, my gosh! This was like something I had seen on television or in storybooks. I made my reservations, boarded the plane, and flew to Washington with my two friends. It was like being in the "Twilight Zone." The trip wasn't even the half of it. When we went inside the White House, I was stupefied by the elaborate hor deurves and sculptured ice centerpiece. It was a beautiful eagle. Yes, an eagle. I just stared at it. I stared at it for a long, long, time. A little while later, I walked into another room which had a microphone set up. A red velvet rope defined the boundary. As I looked around, people began to gather, and suddenly the crowd pushed me up to the rope separating the microphone from the audience. The next thing I knew, President Bill Clinton was standing right in front of the microphone, just a few feet from my face. In my heart I heard a whisper, "Do you see a man [woman] whose work pleaseth the Lord? He [she] shall stand before kings" (Proverbs 22:29). How could this really be happening to me, an ordinary teacher from an ordinary school, in an ordinary American community? After the President of the United States congratulated all of us, he spoke about how much he valued our work and the dedication we had to students across America. Then he began to move through the crowd row by row, shaking our hands and congratulating each teacher. Who on earth would have thought that an ordinary person like me would have been standing in that room that day, let alone in the front row?

God, that's who. Yep. Eagle and all. I began to realize that God has a terrific sense of delight in surprising His kids and a great eye for details. Since one of the ladies I was traveling with was a devout atheist, and the other one was a stranger, I just kept all these wondrous things locked in my heart until I could get home. Even then, I only had enough guts to tell Gail and Donna. The rest of the world would never have believed it. It really happened. The American dream was alive and well. I shared my story over the years, and each time I am amazed at the power of God's amazing grace and faithfulness. He has brought me through the depths of confusions, despair, and discouragement over and over again. Yes, there is a plan. Ask me how I know.

"Amazing grace, how sweet . . .".

The music swells to a crescendo as the Maestro lifts his baton, then drifts into sweet illumination. The end is the beginning of the symphony. No one but He could have written the score. No one but He knows the secrets of the soul. As the heartaches, struggles, life lessons, and victories unfolded over decades, I kept wondering about the melody and the magic of God's love and the mystery of the iris.

My life had never been easy. My sisters and I have shared very painful memories of our own tumultuous family life. For many, many years, my younger sister Patti and my father had chosen to cut me and our youngest sister Susie out of their lives. I had made attempts to reconcile, only to be warned "Just leave us both alone!" When my father lay dying, I went to visit him in the hospital. Painful bladder cancer and emphysema had taken its toll. After a very few minutes, he told me to leave before Patti found out I was there." I don't want any fights," was all he said to me. All that is another story. Then, a few years later, my sister Patti's life came to an abrupt end. When Patti died, her house had to be sorted out, and in the garage were barrels and boxes of treasures from long ago. My other sister, Lloydene, was the only one who had kept any contact with Patti after my father's death. I was amazed at all my dad had kept over all those long, lonely years. Slowly sorting through a ton of odds and ends, my sister uncovered old photographs of our family. She asked me if I wanted to have some of them, in hopes we could still identify some of the people who were part of our early lives. Most precious were the ones of my father and mother taken just before he was sent to the Pacific during World War II. Then unfolding a double picture frame, I came upon a picture of myself as a child. Awe swept my breath away. There was a precious little girl all decked out in an adorable yellow dress. Matching yellow ribbons tenderly adorned her hair, and a baby locket whispered love. There on the bright yellow dress, right over her tiny little heart were two little hand-embroidered flowers. Purple irises.

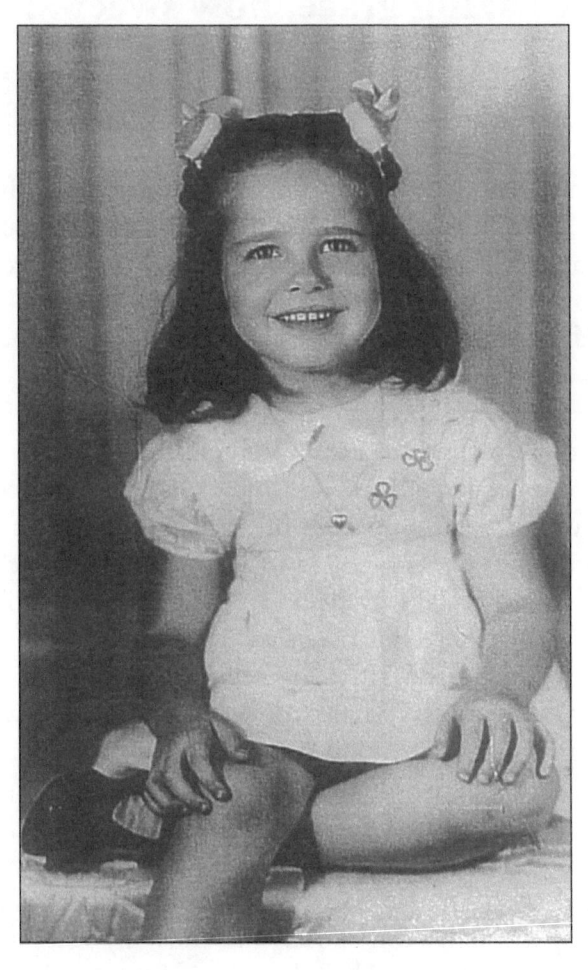

Believe

Works Cited

Berry, Susan. *Irises*. Philadelphia, Pennsylvania: Running Press, 1992. Print.

Blackadder, Elizabeth and Deborah Kellaway. *Iris and Other Flowers:* New York. Harry N. Abrams Incorporated, 1995.Print.

Gordon, Lesley. *The Mystery and Magic of Flowers*. Web & Bower Publishers Limited,1985. Print.

The Holy Bible. Revised Standard Version. New York. Thomas Nelson & Sons. 1952. Print.

www.ingramcontent.com/pod-product-compliance
Lightning Source LLC
LaVergne TN
LVHW041540070526
838199LV00046B/1766